H. P. Lovecraft with Frank Belknap Long's cat Felis

The
H. P. Lovecraft
Cat Book

Edited by S. T. Joshi
Illustrated by Jason C. Eckhardt

Necronomicon Press 2019

"For Susan . . . "

By permission of the estate of H. P. Lovecraft,
Robert C. Harrall, Administrator

Published by Necronomicon Press
P. O. Box 1304, West Warwick, RI 02893 USA
http://www.necropress.com

First edition
ISBN 978-0-940884-98-4 (hardcover)
ISBN 978-0-940884-99-1 (trade paperback)

Contents

Introduction

To say that H. P. Lovecraft was a cat-lover—or, to use the neo-Greek term he may have coined, an ailurophile—would be an understatement. From earliest infancy he appears to have been devoted to the graceful species of felines, whereas he expressed only indifference toward canines. Cats appear in various but always charming ways throughout his fiction, poetry, essays, and letters, and this book is the first to gather the totality of his writings on cats*—to which are added the inimitable illustrations of longtime Lovecraftian artist Jason C. Eckhardt.

It is not at all surprising that Lovecraft—the austere intellectual whose natural reserve and dignity did not impede his ability to enjoy himself in word and deed—would naturally gravitate toward cats. As he writes in his immortal essay, "Cats and Dogs" (1926; first published as "Something about Cats"), "The dog is a peasant and the cat is a gentleman." In his childhood he was given a cat that he named Nigger-Man (a common name for black cats at the time), and the love he felt for that cat is perhaps reflected in a poignant line from "The Cats of Ulthar," telling of the orphan Menes: "when one is very young, one can find great relief in the antics of a black kitten." Lovecraft wasn't exactly an orphan, but his father had died when he was eight and his mother exhibited toward him

---

* Strangely enough, an Italian book on the subject has been published: *Il libro dei gatti*, edited by Gianfranco de Turris and Claudio De Nardi (Rimini: Il Cerchio, 1996). And while it does include some of the material contained in this book, its selection of extracts from Lovecraft's letters is not nearly as comprehensive as the selection found here.

a strange and psychological damaging mixture of emotional aloofness and overprotective coddling. So the young Lovecraft must have found comfort in the "antics" of Nigger-Man. When his family was forced to move out of the lavish family home at 454 Angell Street in Providence, R.I., to a smaller house at 598 Angell Street, nothing could have symbolised the loss of his birthplace than the vanishing of Nigger-Man, who ran away at this time and was never seen again. He was the only pet Lovecraft ever owned. It is no accident that the protagonist of "The Rats in the Walls" (1923) has a cat of this name—and it plays a central role in the development of the narrative.

Lovecraft's first literary expression of his ailurophilia was "The Cats of Ulthar" (1920), whose inspiration had come to him in a dream. Lovecraft was at this time in the midst of his discovery of the work of Lord Dunsany, whose fantasy tales enraptured him when he stumbled upon them in 1919. "The Cats of Ulthar" closely resembles the sardonic tales of tit-for-tat vengeance found in Dunsany's *The Book of Wonder* (1912), although Dunsany (who preferred dogs to cats) wrote no tale on this subject.

Lovecraft was also fond of embodying his love of cats in poetry—and he knew that there was a long tradition of portraying felines in verse, from at least as early as Thomas Gray's "Ode on the Death of a Favourite Cat" (1748).[*] Indeed, Lovecraft's very first discussion of cats in any creative work appears to be a brief passage in the poem "The Bookstall" (1916):

> Upon the floor, in Sol's enfeebled blaze,
> The coal-black puss with youthful ardour plays;

---

[*] See also Antrim Crawford Nelson's anthology *Cats in Prose and Verse* (1947), which contains HPL's "Little Sam Perkins."

Yet what more ancient symbol may we scan
Than puss, the age-long satellite of Man?
Egyptian days a feline worship knew,
And Roman consuls heard the plaintive mew:
The glossy mite can win a scholar's glance,
Whilst sages pause to watch a kitten prance.

When Lovecraft began associating with his friends and colleagues in the amateur journalism movement, he took to writing poems about their pet cats. He soon became notorious for his ailurophily, as W. Paul Cook's famous anecdote relates:

> Belonging as I did to the lowest class of the downtrodden proletariat, I was obliged to go to menial labor in the morning, and so had to cut the session short about midnight. I left Howard sitting at my desk in the study, with the kitten curled up happily in his lap. The kitten, a part Angora, was an unusually independent, self-centred, cold-blooded member of his tribe, but had yielded to Howard's blandishments in spite of the fact that it had been referred to as "a member of the *Felidae.*" I gave it the credit for having the prescience that for that night, at least, it could escape banishment to the basement.
>
> About half-past six in the morning, before going down to breakfast, I poked my head in the study door. There sat Howard, in the same pose in which I had left him six hours before, eyes heavy but head unbowed, with the kitten apparently unmoved.
>
> "Good Lord!" I exclaimed, "haven't you been to bed?"

"No," said Howard, "I didn't want to disturb kitty."

Now I am myself a cat-lover. There is one at this moment curled up on the pile of paper on the desk, and I must extract from under it the next sheet I use. And I will at any time share my last mouse with one. But I question if I would act as nursemaid for a perfectly healthy cat to the extent of sitting up all night with it. Sickness is another thing—the old lodge-brother stuff.[*]

Other amateur journalists soon gained firsthand knowledge of Lovecraft's devotion to felines. Charles W. "Tryout" Smith of Haverhill, Massachusetts, was the editor of the long-running (and typographically challenged) journal *The Tryout*, where "The Cats of Ulthar" had appeared in November 1920. Smith had a cat named Sir Thomas Tryout, whom Lovecraft immortalised in a poem of 1921.

Lovecraft's travels to and residence in New York City, beginning in 1922, exposed him to the numerous stray or domesticated cats in that metropolis. Foremost among them was Frank Belknap Long's haughty cat Felis (the Latin word for cat), whom Lovecraft memoralised not in a formal poem but in one of the many versified Christmas greetings he sent to friends and family over the years. During his first visit to New York, in the fall of 1922, he and Samuel Loveman were staying in the apartment of Sonia H. Greene, whom Lovecraft would marry in 1924. Sonia relates a famous incident with a cat:

> My neighbor who so kindly made room for me had a beautiful Persian cat which she brought to my apartment. As soon as H. P. saw that cat he made "love" to it. He seemed to have a language that the feline brother

[*] W. Paul Cook, *In Memoriam: Howard Phillips Lovecraft* (1941).

understood, for it curled right up in his lap and purred contentedly.

Half in earnest, half in jest I remarked, "What a lot of perfectly good affection to waste on a mere cat, when some woman might highly appreciate it!" His retort was, "How can any woman love a face like mine?" My counter-retort was, "A mother can and some who are not mothers would not have to try very hard." We all laughed while Felis was enjoying some more stroking.[**]

Lovecraft's letters to his aunts, Lillian D. Clark and Annie E. P. Gamwell, are chock full of encounters with various cats on the streets of New York, Brooklyn, and other parts of the metropolitan area; he met them especially in the course of his all-night walking sessions with members of the Kalem Club when he lived in Brooklyn (1924–26) during his brief marriage to Sonia. And it was in February 1925 that he wrote the memorable poem "The Cats," one of the few instances where he mingled his love of cats with his penchant for supernatural horror.

Soon after his return to Providence, Lovecraft wrote his brilliant essay "Cats of Dogs," a delightful fusion of philosophical playfulness and literary virtuosity unlike anything he ever wrote. The essay was a contribution to a discussion on the subject held by the Blue Pencil Club, an amateur journalists' group in Brooklyn; because Lovecraft could not attend the session in person, he sent along the essay, which was probably read to the group by James F. Morton. Lovecraft also embodied his love of cats in a striking passage in *The Dream-Quest of Unknown Kadath* (1926–27), reprinted here. Far from

---

[**] Sonia H. Davis, *The Private Life of H. P. Lovecraft* (1985).

being merely cute and cuddly, felines here are depicted as valiant warriors who defeat the loathsome zoogs in a ferocious battle.

Back in Providence, Lovecraft was thrilled to see an ancient cat—whom he had known since as early as 1906—still surviving at a market on Thomas Street, near his apartment house. The cat lived until at least 1928. It was in 1928 that Lovecraft made a pilgrimage to Wilbraham, Massachusetts, to visit an old amateur colleague, Edith Miniter, to whose menagerie of cats and dogs Lovecraft later paid tribute in a series of poems entitled "Veteropinguis Redivivus."

When, in the spring of 1933, he moved to 66 College Street—an apartment building owned by Brown University and situated on Brown's "fraternity row"—Lovecraft was delighted to discover that the boarding house neighbouring his house had a shed where the cats of the area liked to sun themselves and otherwise cavort in peace and safety. He frequently "borrowed" one or more of these felines, inviting them into his own study, where they would gorge on catnip or play with his rapidly moving pen as he wrote letters. But the presence of these lovely creatures also led to some heartache for Lovecraft; in particular, the lamentable fate of "Little Sam Perkins," born in June and dead by September, inspired him to write one of his most moving elegies, a two-stanza poem that poignantly depicts the grief Lovecraft felt at the untimely passing of this coal-black kitten. Other cats in the "Kappa Alpha Tau" fraternity also suffered sad fates.

Lovecraft kept his correspondents entertained with the doings of the local felidae, while always maintaining interest in the similar activities of his friends' pets all across the country. There was Clark Ashton Smith's cats, Simaetha and General Tabasco; E. Hoffmann Price's cat Nimrod; Duane W.

Rimel's cat Crom (whom Lovecraft apparently named); and, most of all, the numerous cats—High, Low, Jack, Doodlebug, Cyrus, Darius, and others—in the rural home of R. H. Barlow in Florida. The passages in Lovecraft's letters where he discusses these creatures are among the most heartwarming in all his correspondence, showing that Lovecraft was a man of playful whimsy and tender emotions as well as of towering intellect.

The cat has been an object of devotion since at least ancient Egyptian times, when the cat-goddess Bast was widely worshipped. But in our day, few have exhibited the level of ailurophily found in the mind and heart of H. P. Lovecraft. In prose and verse alike, he has perfectly captured the multifarious and at times paradoxical characteristics—beauty and strength, grace and cunning, dignity and unaffected devotion—of the eternally fascinating and eternally mysterious cat.

—S. T. Joshi

The Cats of Ulthar

It is said that in Ulthar, which lies beyond the river Skai, no man may kill a cat; and this I can verily believe as I gaze upon him who sitteth purring before the fire. For the cat is cryptic, and close to strange things which men cannot see. He is the soul of antique Ægyptus, and bearer of tales from forgotten cities in Meröe and Ophir. He is the kin of the jungle's lords, and heir to the secrets of hoary and sinister Africa. The Sphinx is his cousin, and he speaks her language; but he is more ancient than the Sphinx, and remembers that which she hath forgotten.

In Ulthar, before ever the burgesses forbade the killing of cats, there dwelt an old cotter and his wife who delighted to trap and slay the cats of their neighbours. Why they did this I know not; save that many hate the voice of the cat in the night, and take it ill that cats should run stealthily about yards and gardens at twilight. But whatever the reason, this old man and woman took pleasure in trapping and slaying every cat which came near to their hovel; and from some of the sounds heard after dark, many villagers fancied that the manner of slaying was exceedingly peculiar. But the villagers did not discuss such things with the old man and his wife; because of the habitual expression on the withered faces of the two, and because their cottage was so small and so darkly hidden under spreading oaks at the back of a neglected yard. In truth, much as the owners of cats hated these odd folk, they feared them more; and instead of berating them as brutal assassins, merely took care that no cherished pet or mouser should stray toward the remote hovel under the dark trees. When through some unavoidable oversight a cat was missed, and sounds heard after dark, the loser would lament impotently; or console himself by thanking Fate that it was not one of his children who had thus vanished. For the people of Ulthar were simple, and knew not whence it is all cats first came.

One day a caravan of strange wanderers from the South entered the narrow cobbled streets of Ulthar. Dark wanderers they were, and unlike the other roving folk who passed through the village twice every year. In the market-place they told fortunes for silver, and bought gay beads from the merchants. What was the land of these wanderers none could tell; but it was seen that they were given to strange prayers, and that they had painted on the sides of their wagons strange figures with human bodies and the heads of cats, hawks, rams, and lions. And the leader of the caravan wore a head-dress with two horns and a curious disc betwixt the horns.

There was in this singular caravan a little boy with no father or mother, but only a tiny black kitten to cherish. The plague had not been kind to him, yet had left him this small furry thing to mitigate his sorrow; and when one is very young, one can find great relief in the lively antics of a black kitten. So the boy whom the dark people called Menes smiled more often than he wept as he sate playing with his graceful kitten on the steps of an oddly painted wagon.

On the third morning of the wanderers' stay in Ulthar, Menes could not find his kitten; and as he sobbed aloud in the market-place certain villagers told him of the old man and his wife, and of sounds heard in the night. And when he heard these things his sobbing gave place to meditation, and finally to prayer. He stretched out his arms toward the sun and prayed in a tongue no villager could understand; though indeed the villagers did not try very hard to understand, since their attention was mostly taken up by the sky and the odd shapes the clouds were assuming. It was very peculiar, but as the little boy uttered his petition there seemed to form overhead the shadowy, nebulous figures of exotic things; of hybrid creatures crowned with horn-flanked discs. Nature is full of such illusions to impress the imaginative.

That night the wanderers left Ulthar, and were never seen again. And the householders were troubled when they noticed that in all the village there was not a cat to be found. From each hearth the familiar cat had vanished; cats large and small, black, grey, striped, yellow, and white. Old Kranon, the burgomaster, swore that the dark folk had taken the cats away in revenge for the killing of Menes' kitten; and cursed the caravan and the little boy. But Nith, the lean notary, declared that the old cotter and his wife were more likely persons to suspect; for their hatred of cats was notorious and increasingly bold. Still, no one durst complain to the sinister couple; even when little Atal, the innkeeper's son, vowed that he had at twilight seen all the cats of Ulthar in that accursed yard under the trees, pacing very slowly and solemnly in a circle around the cottage, two abreast, as if in performance of some unheard-of rite of beasts. The villagers did not know how much to believe from so small a boy; and though they feared that the evil pair had charmed the cats to their death, they preferred not to chide the old cotter till they met him outside his dark and repellent yard.

So Ulthar went to sleep in vain anger; and when the people awaked at dawn—behold! every cat was back at his accustomed hearth! Large and small, black, grey, striped, yellow, and white, none was missing. Very sleek and fat did the cats appear, and sonorous with purring content. The citizens talked with one another of the affair, and marvelled not a little. Old Kranon again insisted that it was the dark folk who had taken them, since cats did not return alive from the cottage of the ancient man and his wife. But all agreed on one thing: that the refusal of all the cats to eat their portions of meat or drink their saucers of milk was exceedingly curious. And for two whole days the sleek, lazy cats of Ulthar would touch no food, but only doze by the fire or in the sun.

It was fully a week before the villagers noticed that no lights were appearing at dusk in the windows of the cottage under the trees. Then the lean Nith remarked that no one had seen the old man or his wife since the night the cats were away. In another week the burgomaster decided to overcome his fears and call at the strangely silent dwelling as a matter of duty, though in so doing he was careful to take with him Shang the blacksmith and Thul the cutter of stone as witnesses. And when they had broken down the frail door they found only this: two cleanly picked human skeletons on the earthen floor, and a number of singular beetles crawling in the shadowy corners.

There was subsequently much talk among the burgesses of Ulthar. Zath, the coroner, disputed at length with Nith, the lean notary; and Kranon and Shang and Thul were overwhelmed with questions. Even little Atal, the innkeeper's son, was closely questioned and given a sweetmeat as reward. They talked of the old cotter and his wife, of the caravan of dark wanderers, of small Menes and his black kitten, of the prayer of Menes and of the sky during that prayer, of the doings of the cats on the night the caravan left, and of what was later found in the cottage under the dark trees in the repellent yard.

And in the end the burgesses passed that remarkable law which is told of by traders in Hatheg and discussed by travellers in Nir; namely, that in Ulthar no man may kill a cat.

Sir Thomas Tryout

Died Nov. 15, 1921

To the venerable cat of a quaint gentleman in His Majesty's
Province of yᵉ Massachusetts-Bay, who publishes an amateur
magazine call'd *The Tryout*.

The autumn hearth is strangely cold
    Despite the leaping flame,
And all the cheer that shone of old
    Seems lessen'd, dull'd, and tame.

For on the rug where lately doz'd
    A small and furry form,
An empty space is now disclos'd,
    That no mere blaze can warm.

The frosty plain and woodland walk
    In equal sadness sigh
For one who may no longer stalk
    With sylvan hunter's eye.

And if as olden Grecians tell,
    Amidst the thickets deep
A host of fauns and dryads dwell,
    I know that they must weep.

Must weep when autumn twilight brings
      Its mem'ries quaint to view,
Of all the little playful things
      That TOM was wont to do.

So tho' the busy world may pass
      With ne'er a tearful sign
The tiny mound of struggling grass
      Beneath the garden vine,

There's many an eye that fills tonight,
      And many a pensive strain
That sounds for him who stole from sight
      In the November rain.

No sage can trace his soul's advance,
      Or say it lives at all,
For Death against our curious glance
      Has rear'd a mighty wall.

Yet tender Fancy fain would stray
      To fair Hesperian bow'rs,
Where TOM may always purr and play
      Amidst the sun and flow'rs.

The Rats in the Walls

On July 16, 1923, I moved into Exham Priory after the last workman had finished his labours. The restoration had been a stupendous task, for little had remained of the deserted pile but a shell-like ruin; yet because it had been the seat of my ancestors I let no expense deter me. The place had not been inhabited since the reign of James the First, when a tragedy of intensely hideous, though largely unexplained, nature had struck down the master, five of his children, and several servants; and driven forth under a cloud of suspicion and terror the third son, my lineal progenitor and the only survivor of the abhorred line. With this sole heir denounced as a murderer, the estate had reverted to the crown, nor had the accused man made any attempt to exculpate himself or regain his property. Shaken by some horror greater than that of conscience or the law, and expressing only a frantic wish to exclude the ancient edifice from his sight and memory, Walter de la Poer, eleventh Baron Exham, fled to Virginia and there founded the family which by the next century had become known as Delapore.

Exham Priory had remained untenanted, though later allotted to the estates of the Norrys family and much studied because of its peculiarly composite architecture; an architecture involving Gothic towers resting on a Saxon or Romanesque substructure, whose foundation in turn was of a still earlier order or blend of orders—Roman, and even Druidic or native Cymric, if legends speak truly. This foundation was a very singular thing, being merged on one side with the solid limestone of the precipice from whose brink the priory overlooked a desolate valley three miles west of the village of Anchester. Architects and antiquarians loved to examine this strange relic of forgotten centuries, but the country folk hated it. They had hated it hundreds of years before, when my ancestors lived there, and they hated it now, with the moss and mould of abandonment on it. I had not been a day in An-

chester before I knew I came of an accursed house. And this week workmen have blown up Exham Priory, and are busy obliterating the traces of its foundations.

The bare statistics of my ancestry I had always known, together with the fact that my first American forbear had come to the colonies under a strange cloud. Of details, however, I had been kept wholly ignorant through the policy of reticence always maintained by the Delapores. Unlike our planter neighbours, we seldom boasted of crusading ancestors or other mediaeval and Renaissance heroes; nor was any kind of tradition handed down except what may have been recorded in the sealed envelope left before the Civil War by every squire to his eldest son for posthumous opening. The glories we cherished were those achieved since the migration; the glories of a proud and honourable, if somewhat reserved and unsocial Virginia line.

During the war our fortunes were extinguished and our whole existence changed by the burning of Carfax, our home on the banks of the James. My grandfather, advanced in years, had perished in that incendiary outrage, and with him the envelope that bound us all to the past. I can recall that fire today as I saw it then at the age of seven, with the Federal soldiers shouting, the women screaming, and the negroes howling and praying. My father was in the army, defending Richmond, and after many formalities my mother and I were passed through the lines to join him. When the war ended we all moved north, whence my mother had come; and I grew to manhood, middle age, and ultimate wealth as a stolid Yankee. Neither my father nor I ever knew what our hereditary envelope had contained, and as I merged into the greyness of Massachusetts business life I lost all interest in the mysteries which evidently lurked far back in my family tree. Had I suspected their nature, how gladly I would have left Exham Priory to its moss, bats, and cobwebs!

My father died in 1904, but without any message to

leave me, or to my only child, Alfred, a motherless boy of ten. It was this boy who reversed the order of family information; for although I could give him only jesting conjectures about the past, he wrote me of some very interesting ancestral legends when the late war took him to England in 1917 as an aviation officer. Apparently the Delapores had a colourful and perhaps sinister history, for a friend of my son's, Capt. Edward Norrys of the Royal Flying Corps, dwelt near the family seat at Anchester and related some peasant superstitions which few novelists could equal for wildness and incredibility. Norrys himself, of course, did not take them seriously; but they amused my son and made good material for his letters to me. It was this legendry which definitely turned my attention to my transatlantic heritage, and made me resolve to purchase and restore the family seat which Norrys shewed to Alfred in its picturesque desertion, and offered to get for him at a surprisingly reasonable figure, since his own uncle was the present owner.

I bought Exham Priory in 1918, but was almost immediately distracted from my plans of restoration by the return of my son as a maimed invalid. During the two years that he lived I thought of nothing but his care, having even placed my business under the direction of partners. In 1921, as I found myself bereaved and aimless, a retired manufacturer no longer young, I resolved to divert my remaining years with my new possession. Visiting Anchester in December, I was entertained by Capt. Norrys, a plump, amiable young man who had thought much of my son, and secured his assistance in gathering plans and anecdotes to guide in the coming restoration. Exham Priory itself I saw without emotion, a jumble of tottering mediaeval ruins covered with lichens and honeycombed with rooks' nests, perched perilously upon a precipice, and denuded of floors or other interior features save the stone walls of the separate towers.

As I gradually recovered the image of the edifice as it had been when my ancestor left it over three centuries before, I began to hire workmen for the reconstruction. In every case I was forced to go outside the immediate locality, for the Anchester villagers had an almost unbelievable fear and hatred of the place. This sentiment was so great that it was sometimes communicated to the outside labourers, causing numerous desertions; whilst its scope appeared to include both the priory and its ancient family.

My son had told me that he was somewhat avoided during his visits because he was a de la Poer, and I now found myself subtly ostracised for a like reason until I convinced the peasants how little I knew of my heritage. Even then they sullenly disliked me, so that I had to collect most of the village traditions through the mediation of Norrys. What the people could not forgive, perhaps, was that I had come to restore a symbol so abhorrent to them; for, rationally or not, they viewed Exham Priory as nothing less than a haunt of fiends and werewolves.

Piecing together the tales which Norrys collected for me, and supplementing them with the accounts of several savants who had studied the ruins, I deduced that Exham Priory stood on the site of a prehistoric temple; a Druidical or ante-Druidical thing which must have been contemporary with Stonehenge. That indescribable rites had been celebrated there, few doubted; and there were unpleasant tales of the transference of these rites into the Cybele-worship which the Romans had introduced. Inscriptions still visible in the sub-cellar bore such unmistakable letters as "DIV . . . OPS . . . MAGNA. MAT . . . " sign of the Magna Mater whose dark worship was once vainly forbidden to Roman citizens. Anchester had been the camp of the third Augustan legion, as many remains attest, and it was said that the temple of Cybele was splendid and thronged with worshippers who performed nameless ceremonies at the bidding of a Phrygian priest. Tales added that the fall of the old religion did not end the orgies at the temple, but that the priests lived on in the new faith without real change. Likewise was it said that the rites did not vanish with the Roman power, and that certain among the Saxons added to what remained of the temple, and gave it the essential outline it subsequently preserved, making it the centre of a cult feared through half the heptarchy. About 1000 A.D. the place is mentioned in a chronicle as being a substantial stone priory housing a strange and powerful monastic order and surrounded by extensive gardens which needed no walls to exclude a frightened populace. It was never destroyed by the Danes, though after the Norman Conquest it must have declined tremendously; since there was no impediment when Henry the Third granted the site to my ancestor, Gilbert de la Poer, First Baron Exham, in 1261.

Of my family before this date there is no evil report, but something strange must have happened then. In one chronicle there is a reference to a de la Poer as "cursed of God" in 1307, whilst village legendry had nothing but evil and frantic fear to tell of the castle that went up on the foundations of the old temple and priory. The fireside tales were of the most grisly description, all the ghastlier because of their frightened reticence and cloudy evasiveness. They represented my ancestors as a race of hereditary daemons beside whom Gilles de Retz and the Marquis de Sade would seem the veriest tyros, and hinted whisperingly at their responsibility for the occasional disappearances of villagers through several generations.

The worst characters, apparently, were the barons and their direct heirs; at least, most was whispered about these. If of healthier inclinations, it was said, an heir would early and mysteriously die to make way for another more typical scion. There seemed to be an inner cult in the family, presided over by the head of the house, and sometimes closed except to a few members. Temperament rather than ancestry was evidently the basis of this cult, for it was entered by several who married into the family. Lady Margaret Trevor from Cornwall, wife of Godfrey, the second son of the fifth baron, became a favourite bane of children all over the countryside, and the daemon heroine of a particularly horrible old ballad not yet extinct near the Welsh border. Preserved in balladry, too, though not illustrating the same point, is the hideous tale of Lady Mary de la Poer, who shortly after her marriage to the Earl of Shrewsfield was killed by him and his mother, both of the slayers being absolved and blessed by the priest to whom they confessed what they dared not repeat to the world.

These myths and ballads, typical as they were of crude superstition, repelled me greatly. Their persistence, and their application to so long a line of my ancestors, were especially annoying; whilst the imputations of monstrous habits proved unpleasantly reminiscent of the one known scandal of my immediate forbears—the case of my cousin, young Randolph Delapore of Carfax, who went among the negroes and became a voodoo priest after he returned from the Mexican War.

I was much less disturbed by the vaguer tales of wails and howlings in the barren, windswept valley beneath the limestone cliff; of the graveyard stenches after the spring rains; of the floundering, squealing white thing on which Sir John Clave's horse had trod one night in a lonely field; and of the servant who had gone mad at what he saw in the priory in the full light of day. These things were hackneyed spectral lore, and I was at that time a pronounced sceptic. The accounts of vanished peasants were less to be dismissed, though not especially significant in view of mediaeval custom. Prying curiosity meant death, and more than one severed head had been publicly shewn on the bastions—now effaced—around Exham Priory.

A few of the tales were exceedingly picturesque, and made me wish I had learnt more of comparative mythology in my youth. There was, for instance, the belief that a legion of bat-winged devils kept Witches' Sabbath each night at the priory—a legion whose sustenance might explain the disproportionate abundance of coarse vegetables harvested in the vast gardens. And, most vivid of all, there was the dramatic epic of the rats—the scampering army of obscene vermin which had burst forth from the castle three months after the tragedy that doomed it to desertion—the lean, filthy, ravenous army which had swept all before it and devoured fowl, cats, dogs, hogs, sheep, and even two hapless human beings before its fury was spent. Around that unforgettable rodent army a whole separate cycle of myths revolves, for it scattered among the village homes and brought curses and horrors in its train.

Such was the lore that assailed me as I pushed to completion, with an elderly obstinacy, the work of restoring my ancestral home. It must not be imagined for a moment that these tales formed my principal psychological environment. On the other hand, I was constantly praised and encouraged by Capt. Norrys and the antiquarians who surrounded and aided me. When the task was done, over two years after its commencement, I viewed the great rooms, wainscotted walls, vaulted ceilings, mullioned windows, and broad staircases with a pride which fully compensated for the prodigious expense of the restoration. Every attribute of the Middle Ages was cunningly reproduced, and the new parts blended perfectly with the original walls and foundations. The seat of my fathers was complete, and I looked forward to redeeming at last the local fame of the line which ended in me. I would reside here permanently, and prove that a de la Poer (for I had adopted again the original spelling of the name) need not be a fiend. My comfort was perhaps augmented by the fact that, although Exham Priory was mediaevally fitted, its interior was in truth wholly new and free from old vermin and old ghosts alike.

As I have said, I moved in on July 16, 1923. My household consisted of seven servants and nine cats, of which latter species I am particularly fond. My eldest cat, "Nigger-Man", was seven years old and had come with me from my home in Bolton, Massachusetts; the others I had accumulated whilst living with Capt. Norrys' family during the restoration of the priory. For five days our routine proceeded with the utmost placidity, my time being spent mostly in the codification of old family data. I had now obtained some very circumstantial accounts of the final tragedy and flight of Walter de la Poer, which I conceived to be the probable contents of the hereditary paper lost in the fire at Carfax. It appeared that my ancestor was accused with much reason of having killed all the other members of his household, except four servant confederates, in their sleep, about two weeks after a shocking discovery which changed his whole demeanour, but which, except by implication, he disclosed to no one save perhaps the servants who assisted him and afterward fled beyond reach.

This deliberate slaughter, which included a father, three brothers, and two sisters, was largely condoned by the villagers, and so slackly treated by the law that its per-petrator escaped honoured, unharmed, and undisguised to Virginia; the general whispered sentiment being that he had purged the land of an immemorial curse. What discovery had prompted an act so terrible, I could scarcely even conjecture. Walter de la Poer must have known for years the sinister tales about his family, so that this material could have given him no fresh impulse. Had he, then, witnessed some appalling ancient rite, or stumbled upon some frightful and revealing symbol in the priory or its vicinity? He was reputed to have been a shy, gentle youth in England. In Virignia he seemed not so much hard or bitter as harassed and apprehensive. He was spoken of in the diary of another gentleman-adventurer, Francis Harley of Bellview, as a man of unexampled justice, honour, and delicacy.

On July 22 occurred the first incident which, though lightly dismissed at the time, takes on a preternatural signif-icance in relation to later events. It was so simple as to be al-most negligible, and could not possibly have been noticed un-der the circumstances; for it must be recalled that since I was in a building practically fresh and new except for the walls, and surrounded by a well-balanced staff of servitors, appre-hension would have been absurd despite the locality. What I afterward remembered is merely this—that my old black cat, whose moods I know so well, was undoubtedly alert and anx-ious to an extent wholly out of keeping with his natural char-acter. He roved from room to room, restless and disturbed, and sniffed constantly about the walls which formed part of the old Gothic structure. I realise how trite this sounds—like the inevitable dog in the ghost story, which always growls before his master sees the sheeted figure—yet I cannot consis-tently suppress it.

The following day a servant complained of restlessness among all the cats in the house. He came to me in my study, a lofty west room on the second story, with groined arches, black oak panelling, and a triple Gothic window overlooking the limestone cliff and desolate valley; and even as he spoke I saw the jetty form of Nigger-Man creeping along the west wall and scratching at the new panels which overlaid the ancient stone. I told the man that there must be some singular odour or emanation from the old stonework, imperceptible to human senses, but affecting the delicate organs of cats even through the new woodwork. This I truly believed, and when the fellow suggested the presence of mice or rats, I mentioned that there had been no rats there for three hundred years, and that even the field mice of the surrounding country could hardly be found in these high walls, where they had never been known to stray. That afternoon I called on Capt. Norrys, and he assured me that it would be quite incredible for field mice to infest the priory in such a sudden and unprecedented fashion.

That night, dispensing as usual with a valet, I retired in the west tower chamber which I had chosen as my own, reached from the study by a stone staircase and short gallery—the former partly ancient, the latter entirely restored. This room was circular, very high, and without wainscotting, being hung with arras which I had myself chosen in London. Seeing that Nigger-Man was with me, I shut the heavy Gothic door and retired by the light of the electric bulbs which so cleverly counterfeited candles, finally switching off the light and sinking on the carved and canopied four-poster, with the venerable cat in his accustomed place across my feet. I did not draw the curtains, but gazed out at the narrow north window which I faced. There was a suspicion of aurora in the sky, and the delicate traceries of the window were pleasantly silhouetted.

At some time I must have fallen quietly asleep, for I recall a distinct sense of leaving strange dreams, when the cat started violently from his placid position. I saw him in the faint auroral glow, head strained forward, fore feet on my ankles, and hind feet stretched behind. He was looking intensely at a point on the wall somewhat west of the window, a point which to my eye had nothing to mark it, but toward which all my attention was now directed. And as I watched, I knew that Nigger-Man was not vainly excited. Whether the arras actually moved I cannot say. I think it did, very slightly. But what I can swear to is that behind it I heard a low, distinct scurrying as of rats or mice. In a moment the cat had jumped bodily on the screening tapestry, bringing the affected section to the floor with his weight, and exposing a damp, ancient wall of stone; patched here and there by the restorers, and devoid of any trace of rodent prowlers. Nigger-Man raced up and down the floor by this part of the wall, clawing the fallen arras and seemingly trying at times to insert a paw between the wall and the oaken floor. He found nothing, and after a time returned wearily to his place across my feet. I had not moved, but I did not sleep again that night.

In the morning I questioned all the servants, and found that none of them had noticed anything unusual, save that the cook remembered the actions of a cat which had rested on her windowsill. This cat had howled at some unknown hour of the night, awaking the cook in time for her to see him dart purposefully out of the open door down the stairs. I drowsed away the noontime, and in the afternoon called again on Capt. Norrys, who became exceedingly interested in what I told him. The odd incidents—so slight yet so curious—appealed to his sense of the picturesque, and elicited from him a number of reminiscences of local ghostly lore. We were genuinely perplexed at the presence of rats, and Norrys lent me some traps and Paris green, which I had the servants place in strategic localities when I returned.

I retired early, being very sleepy, but was harassed by dreams of the most horrible sort. I seemed to be looking down from an immense height upon a twilit grotto, knee-deep with filth, where a white-bearded daemon swineherd drove about with his staff a flock of fungous, flabby beasts whose appearance filled me with unutterable loathing. Then, as the swineherd paused and nodded over his task, a mighty swarm of rats rained down on the stinking abyss and fell to devouring beasts and man alike.

From this terrific vision I was abruptly awaked by the motions of Nigger-Man, who had been sleeping as usual across my feet. This time I did not have to question the source of his snarls and hisses, and of the fear which made him sink his claws into my ankle, unconcscious of their effect; for on every side of the chamber the walls were alive with nauseous sound—the verminous slithering of ravenous, gigantic rats. There was now no aurora to shew the state of the arras—the fallen section of which had been replaced—but I was not too frightened to switch on the light.

As the bulbs leapt into radiance I saw a hideous shaking all over the tapestry, causing the somewhat peculiar designs to execute a singular dance of death. This motion disappeared almost at once, and the sound with it. Springing out of bed, I poked at the arras with the long handle of a warming-pan that rested near, and lifted one section to see what lay beneath. There was nothing but the patched stone wall, and even the cat had lost his tense realisation of abnormal pres-

ences. When I examined the circular trap that had been placed in the room, I found all of the openings sprung, though no trace remained of what had been caught and had escaped.

Further sleep was out of the question, so, lighting a candle, I opened the door and went out in the gallery toward the stairs to my study, Nigger-Man following at my heels. Before we had reached the stone steps, however, the cat darted ahead of me and vanished down the ancient flight. As I descended the stairs myself, I became suddenly aware of sounds in the great room below; sounds of a nature which could not be mistaken. The oak-panelled walls were alive with rats, scampering and milling, whilst Nigger-Man was racing about with the fury of a baffled hunter. Reaching the bottom, I switched on the light, which did not this time cause the noise to subside. The rats continued their riot, stampeding with such force and distinctness that I could finally assign to their motions a definite direction. These creatures, in numbers apparently inexhaustible, were engaged in one stupendous migration from inconceivable heights to some depth conceivably, or inconceivably, below.

I now heard steps in the corridor, and in another moment two servants pushed open the massive door. They were searching the house for some unknown source of disturbance which had thrown all the cats into a snarling panic and caused them to plunge precipitately down several flights of stairs and squat, yowling, before the closed door to the sub-cellar. I asked them if they had heard the rats, but they replied in the negative. And when I turned to call their attention to the sounds in the panels, I realised that the noise had ceased. With the two men, I went down to the door of the sub-cellar, but found the cats already dispersed. Later I resolved to explore the crypt below, but for the present I merely made a round of the traps. All were sprung, yet all were tenantless. Satisfying myself that no one had heard the rats save the felines and me, I sat in my study till morning; thinking profoundly, and recalling every scrap of legend I had unearthed concerning the building I inhabited.

I slept some in the forenoon, leaning back in the one comfortable library chair which my mediaeval plan of furnishing could not banish. Later I telephoned to Capt. Norrys, who came over and helped me explore the sub-cellar. Absolutely nothing untoward was found, although we could not repress a thrill at the knowledge that this vault was built by Roman hands. Every low arch and massive pillar was Roman—not the debased Romanesque of the bungling Saxons, but the severe and harmonious classicism of the age of the Caesars; indeed, the walls abounded with inscriptions familiar to the antiquarians who had repeatedly explored the place—things like "P.GETAE. PROP . . . TEMP . . . DONA . . ." and "L. PRAEC . . . VS . . . PONTIFI . . . ATYS . . ."

The reference to Atys made me shiver, for I had read Catullus and knew something of the hideous rites of the Eastern god, whose worship was so mixed with that of Cybele. Norrys and I, by the light of lanterns, tried to interpret the odd and nearly effaced designs on certain irregularly rectangular blocks of stone generally held to be altars, but could make nothing of them. We remembered that one pattern, a sort of rayed sun, was held by students to imply a non-Roman origin, suggesting that these altars had merely been adopted by the Roman priests from some older and perhaps aboriginal temple on the same site. On one of these blocks were some brown stains which made me wonder. The largest, in the centre of the room, had certain features on the upper surface which indicated its connexion with fire—probably burnt offerings.

Such were the sights in that crypt before whose door the cats had howled, and where Norrys and I now determined to pass the night. Couches were brought down by the servants, who were told not to mind any nocturnal actions of the cats, and Nigger-Man was admitted as much for help as for companionship. We decided to keep the great oak door—a modern replica with slits for ventilation—tightly closed; and, with this attended to, we retired with lanterns still burning to await whatever might occur.

The vault was very deep in the foundations of the priory, and undoubtedly far down on the face of the beetling limestone cliff overlooking the waste valley. That it had been the goal of the scuffling and unexplainable rats I could not doubt, though why, I could not tell. As we lay there expectantly, I found my vigil occasionally mixed with half-formed dreams from which the uneasy motions of the cat across my feet would rouse me. These dreams were not wholesome, but horribly like the one I had had the night before. I saw again the twilit grotto, and the swineherd with his unmentionable fungous beasts wallowing in filth, and as I looked at these things they seemed nearer and more distinct—so distinct that I could almost observe their features. Then I did observe the flabby features of one of them—and awaked with such a scream that Nigger-Man started up, whilst Capt. Norrys, who had not slept, laughed considerably. Norrys might have laughed more—or perhaps less—had he known what it was that made me scream. But I did not remember myself till later. Ultimate horror often paralyses memory in a merciful way.

Norrys waked me when the phenomena began. Out of the same frightful dream I was called by his gentle shaking and his urging to listen to the cats. Indeed, there was much to listen to, for beyond the closed door at the head of the stone steps was a veritable nightmare of feline yelling and clawing, whilst Nigger-Man, unmindful of his kindred outside, was running excitedly around the bare stone walls, in which I heard the same babel of scurrying rats that had troubled me the night before.

An acute terror now rose within me, for here were anomalies which nothing normal could well explain. These rats, if not the creatures of a madness which I shared with the cats alone, must be burrowing and sliding in Roman walls I had thought to be of solid limestone blocks . . . unless perhaps the action of water through more than seventeen centuries had eaten winding tunnels which rodent bodies had worn clear and ample. . . . But even so, the spectral horror was no less; for if these were living vermin why did not Norrys hear their disgusting commotion? Why did he urge me to watch Nigger-Man and listen to the cats outside, and why did he guess wildly and vaguely at what could have aroused them?

By the time I had managed to tell him, as rationally as I could, what I thought I was hearing, my ears gave me the last fading impression of the scurrying; which had retreated *still downward*, far underneath this deepest of sub-cellars till it seemed as if the whole cliff below were riddled with questing rats. Norrys was not as sceptical as I had anticipated, but instead seemed profoundly moved. He motioned to me to notice that the cats at the door had ceased their clamour, as if giving up the rats for lost; whilst Nigger-Man had a burst of renewed restlessness, and was clawing frantically around the bottom of the large stone altar in the centre of the room, which was nearer Norrys' couch than mine.

My fear of the unknown was at this point very great. Something astounding had occurred, and I saw that Capt.

Norrys, a younger, stouter, and presumably more naturally materialistic man, was affected fully as much as myself—perhaps because of his lifelong and intimate familiarity with local legend. We could for the moment do nothing but watch the old black cat as he pawed with decreasing fervour at the base of the altar, occasionally looking up and mewing to me in that persuasive manner which he used when he wished me to perform some favour for him.

Norrys now took a lantern close to the altar and examined the place where Nigger-Man was pawing; silently kneeling and scraping away the lichens of centuries which joined the massive pre-Roman block to the tessellated floor. He did not find anything, and was about to abandon his efforts when I noticed a trivial circumstance which made me shudder, even though it implied nothing more than I had already imagined. I told him of it, and we both looked at its almost imperceptible manifestation with the fixedness of fascinated discovery and acknowledgment. It was only this—that the flame of the lantern set down near the altar was slightly but certainly flickering from a draught of air which it had not before received, and which came indubitably from the crevices between floor and altar where Norrys was scraping away the lichens.

We spent the rest of the night in the brilliantly lighted study, nervously discussing what we should do next. The discovery that some vault deeper than the deepest known masonry of the Romans underlay this accursed pile—some vault unsuspected by the curious antiquarians of three centuries—would have been sufficient to excite us without any background of the sinister. As it was, the fascination became twofold; and we paused in doubt whether to abandon our search and quit the priory forever in superstitious caution, or to gratify our sense of adventure and brave whatever horrors

might await us in the unknown depths. By morning we had compromised, and decided to go to London to gather a group of archaeologists and scientific men fit to cope with the mystery. It should be mentioned that before leaving the sub-cellar we had vainly tried to move the central altar which we now recognised as the gate to a new pit of nameless fear. What secret would open the gate, wiser men than we would have to find.

During many days in London Capt. Norrys and I presented our facts, conjectures, and legendary anecdotes to five eminent authorities, all men who could be trusted to respect any family disclosures which future explorations might develop. We found most of them little disposed to scoff, but instead intensely interested and sincerely sympathetic. It is hardly necessary to name them all, but I may say that they included Sir William Brinton, whose excavations in the Troad excited most of the world in their day. As we all took the train for Anchester I felt myself poised on the brink of frightful revelations, a sensation symbolised by the air of mourning among the many Americans at the unexpected death of the President on the other side of the world.

On the evening of August 7th we reached Exham Priory, where the servants assured me that nothing unusual had occurred. The cats, even old Nigger-Man, had been perfectly placid; and not a trap in the house had been sprung. We were to begin exploring on the following day, awaiting which I assigned well-appointed rooms to all my guests. I myself retired in my own tower chamber, with Nigger-Man across my feet. Sleep came quickly, but hideous dreams assailed me. There was a vision of a Roman feast like that of Trimalchio, with a horror in a covered platter. Then came that damnable, recurrent thing about the swineherd and his filthy drove in the twilit grotto. Yet when I awoke it was full daylight, with normal sounds in the house below. The rats, living or spectral, had not troubled me; and Nigger-Man was still quietly asleep. On going down, I found that the same tranquillity had prevailed elsewhere; a condition which one of the assembled savants—a fellow named Thornton, devoted to the psychic—rather absurdly laid to the fact that I had now been shewn the thing which certain forces had wished to shew me.

All was now ready, and at 11 a.m. our entire group of seven men, bearing powerful electric searchlights and implements of excavation, went down to the sub-cellar and bolted the door behind us. Nigger-Man was with us, for the investigators found no occasion to despise his excitability, and were indeed anxious that he be present in case of obscure rodent manifestations. We noted the Roman inscriptions and unknown altar designs only briefly, for three of the savants had already seen them, and all knew their characteristics. Prime attention was paid to the momentous central altar, and within an hour Sir William Brinton had caused it to tilt backward, balanced by some unknown species of counterweight.

There now lay revealed such a horror as would have overwhelmed us had we not been prepared. Through a nearly square opening in the tiled floor, sprawling on a flight of stone steps so prodigiously worn that it was little more than an inclined plane at the centre, was a ghastly array of human or semi-human bones. Those which retained their collocation as skeletons shewed attitudes of panic fear, and over all were the marks of rodent gnawing. The skulls denoted nothing short of utter idiocy, cretinism, or primitive semi-apedom. Above the hellishly littered steps arched a descending passage seemingly chiselled from the solid rock, and conducting a current of air. This current was not a sudden and noxious rush as from a closed vault, but a cool breeze with something of freshness in it. We did not pause long, but shiveringly began to clear a passage down the steps. It was then that Sir William, examining the hewn walls, made the odd observation that the passage, according to the direction of the strokes, must have been chiselled *from beneath*.

I must be very deliberate now, and choose my words.

After ploughing down a few steps amidst the gnawed bones we saw that there was light ahead; not any mystic phosphorescence, but a filtered daylight which could not come except from unknown fissures in the cliff that overlooked the waste valley. That such fissures had escaped notice from outside was hardly remarkable, for not only is the valley wholly uninhabited, but the cliff is so high and beetling that only an aëronaut could study its face in detail. A few steps more, and our breaths were literally snatched from us by what we saw; so literally that Thornton, the psychic investigator, actually fainted in the arms of the dazed man who stood behind him. Norrys, his plump face utterly white and flabby, simply cried out inarticulately; whilst I think that what I did was to gasp or hiss, and cover my eyes. The man behind me—the only one of the party older than I—croaked the hackneyed "My God!" in the most cracked voice I ever heard. Of seven cultivated men, only Sir William Brinton retained his composure; a thing more to his credit because he led the party and must have seen the sight first.

It was a twilit grotto of enormous height, stretching away farther than any eye could see; a subterraneous world of limitless mystery and horrible suggestion. There were buildings and other architectural remains—in one terrified glance I saw a weird pattern of tumuli, a savage circle of monoliths, a low-domed Roman ruin, a sprawling Saxon pile, and an early English edifice of wood—but all these were dwarfed by the ghoulish spectacle presented by the general surface of the ground. For yards about the steps extended an insane tangle of human bones, or bones at least as human as those on the steps. Like a foamy sea they stretched, some fallen apart, but others wholly or partly articulated as skeletons; these latter invariably in postures of daemoniac frenzy, either fighting off some menace or clutching other forms with cannibal intent.

When Dr. Trask, the anthropologist, stooped to classify the skulls, he found a degraded mixture which utterly baffled him. They were mostly lower than the Piltdown man in the scale of evolution, but in every case definitely human. Many were of higher grade, and a very few were the skulls of supremely and sensitively developed types. All the bones were gnawed, mostly by rats, but somewhat by others of the half-human drove. Mixed with them were many tiny bones of rats—fallen members of the lethal army which closed the ancient epic.

I wonder that any man among us lived and kept his sanity through that hideous day of discovery. Not Hoffmann or Huysmans could conceive a scene more wildly incredible, more frenetically repellent, or more Gothically grotesque than the twilit grotto through which we seven staggered; each stumbling on revelation after revelation, and trying to keep for the nonce from thinking of the events which must have taken place there three hundred, or a thousand, or two thousand, or ten thousand years ago. It was the antechamber of hell, and poor Thornton fainted again when Trask told him that some of the skeleton things must have descended as quadrupeds through the last twenty or more generations.

Horror piled on horror as we began to interpret the architectural remains. The quadruped things—with their occasional recruits from the biped class—had been kept in stone pens, out of which they must have broken in their last delirium of hunger or rat-fear. There had been great herds of them, evidently fattened on the coarse vegetables whose remains could be found as a sort of poisonous ensilage at the bottom of huge stone bins older than Rome. I knew now why my ancestors had had such excessive gardens—would to heaven I could forget! The purpose of the herds I did not have to ask.

Sir William, standing with his searchlight in the Roman ruin, translated aloud the most shocking ritual I have ever known; and told of the diet of the antediluvian cult which the priests of Cybele found and mingled with their own. Norrys, used as he was to the trenches, could not walk straight when he came out of the English building. It was a butcher shop and kitchen—he had expected that—but it was too much to see familiar English implements in such a place, and to read familiar English *graffiti* there, some as recent as 1610. I could not go in that building—that building whose daemon activities were stopped only by the dagger of my ancestor Walter de la Poer.

What I did venture to enter was the low Saxon building, whose oaken door had fallen, and there I found a terrible row of ten stone cells with rusty bars. Three had tenants, all skeletons of high grade, and on the bony forefinger of one I found a seal ring with my own coat-of-arms. Sir William found a vault with far older cells below the Roman chapel, but these cells were empty. Below them was a low crypt with cases of formally arranged bones, some of them bearing terrible parallel inscriptions carved in Latin, Greek, and the tongue of Phrygia. Meanwhile, Dr. Trask had opened one of the prehistoric tumuli, and brought to light skulls which were slighty more human than a gorilla's, and which bore indescribable ideographic carvings. Through all this horror my cat stalked unperturbed. Once I saw him monstrously perched atop a mountain of bones, and wondered at the secrets that might lie behind his yellow eyes.

Having grasped to some slight degree the frightful revelations of this twilit area—an area so hideously foreshadowed by my recurrent dream—we turned to that apparently boundless depth of midnight cavern where no ray of light from the cliff could penetrate. We shall never know what sightless Stygian worlds yawn beyond the little distance we went, for it was decided that such secrets are not good for mankind. But there was plenty to engross us close at hand, for we had not gone far before the searchlights shewed that accursed infinity of pits in which the rats had feasted, and whose sudden lack of replenishment had driven the ravenous rodent army first to turn on the living herds of starving things, and then to burst forth from the priory in that historic orgy of devastation which the peasants will never forget.

God! those carrion black pits of sawed, picked bones and opened skulls! Those nightmare chasms choked with the pithecanthropoid, Celtic, Roman, and English bones of countless unhallowed centuries! Some of them were full, and none can say how deep they had once been. Others were still bottomless to our searchlights, and peopled by unnamable fancies. What, I thought, of the hapless rats that stumbled into such traps amidst the blackness of their quests in this grisly Tartarus?

Once my foot slipped near a horribly yawning brink, and I had a moment of ecstatic fear. I must have been musing a long time, for I could not see any of the party but the plump Capt. Norrys. Then there came a sound from that inky, boundless, farther distance that I thought I knew; and I saw my old black cat dart past me like a winged Egyptian god, straight into the illimitable gulf of the unknown. But I was not far behind, for there was no doubt after another second. It was the eldritch scurrying of those fiend-born rats, always questing for new horrors, and determined to lead me on even unto those grinning caverns of earth's centre where Nyarla-thotep, the mad faceless god, howls blindly in the darkness to the piping of two amorphous idiot flute-players.

My searchlight expired, but still I ran. I heard voices, and yowls, and echoes, but above all there gently rose that impious, insidious scurrying; gently rising, rising, as a stiff bloated corpse gently rises above an oily river that flows under endless onyx bridges to a black, putrid sea. Something bumped into me—something soft and plump. It must have been the rats; the viscous, gelatinous, ravenous army that feast on the dead and the living. . . . Why shouldn't rats eat a de la Poer as a de la Poer eats forbidden things? . . . The war ate my boy, damn them all . . . and the Yanks ate Carfax with flames and burnt Grandsire Delapore and the secret . . . No, no, I tell you, I am *not* that daemon swineherd in the twilit grotto! It was *not* Edward Norrys' fat face on that flabby, fungous thing! Who says I am a de la Poer? He lived, but my boy died! . . . Shall a Norrys hold the lands of a de la Poer? . . . It's voodoo, I tell you . . . that spotted snake . . . Curse you, Thornton, I'll teach you to faint at what my family do! . . . 'Sblood, thou stinkard, I'll learn ye how to gust . . . wolde ye swynke me thilke wys? . . . *Magna Mater! Magna Mater! . . . Atys . . . Dia ad aghaidh 's ad aodann . . . agus bas dunach ort! Dhonas 's dholas ort, agus leat-sa! . . . Ungl . . . ungl . . . rrrlh . . . chchch . . .*

That is what they say I said when they found me in the blackness after three hours; found me crouching in the blackness over the plump, half-eaten body of Capt. Norrys, with my own cat leaping and tearing at my throat. Now they have blown up Exham Priory, taken my Nigger-Man away from me, and shut me into this barred room at Hanwell with fearful whispers about my heredity and experiences. Thornton is in the next room, but they prevent me from talking to him. They are trying, too, to suppress most of the facts concerning the priory. When I speak of poor Norrys they accuse me of a hideous thing, but they must know that I did not do it. They must know it was the rats; the slithering, scurrying rats whose scampering will never let me sleep; the daemon rats that race behind the padding in this room and beckon me down to greater horrors than I have ever known; the rats they can never hear; the rats, the rats in the walls.

The Cats

Babels of blocks to the high heavens tow'ring,
      Flumes of futility swirling below;
Poisonous fungi in brick and stone flow'ring,
      Lanterns that shudder and death-lights that glow.

Black monstrous bridges across oily rivers,
      Cobwebs of cable by nameless things spun;
Catacomb deeps whose dank chaos delivers
      Streams of live foetor, that rots in the sun.

Colour and splendour, disease and decaying,
      Shrieking and ringing and scrambling insane,
Rabbles exotic to stranger-gods praying,
      Jumbles of odour that stifle the brain.

Legions of cats from the alleys nocturnal,
      Howling and lean in the glare of the moon,
Screaming the future with mouthings infernal,
      Yelling the burden of Pluto's red rune.

Tall tow'rs and pyramids ivy'd and crumbling,
Bats that swoop low in the weed-cumber'd streets;
Bleak broken bridges o'er rivers whose rumbling
Joins with no voice as the thick tide retreats.

Belfries that blackly against the moon totter,
Caverns whose mouths are by mosses effac'd,
And living to answer the wind and the water,
Only the lean cats that howl in the waste!

In Memoriam:

Oscar Incoul Verelst of Manhattan
1920–1926

Damn'd be this harsh mechanick Age
      That whirls us fast and faster,
And swallows with Sabazian Rage
      Nine Lives in one Disaster.

I take my Quill with sadden'd Thought,
      Tho' falt'ringly I do it;
And, having curst the Juggernaut,
      Inscribe: OSCARVS FVIT!

Cats and Dogs

Being told of the cat-and-dog fight about to occur in the Blue Pencil Club—a new thing for your circle, perhaps, though not unfamiliar to amateurdom as a whole—I cannot resist contributing a few Thomasic yowls and sibilants upon my side of the dispute, though conscious that the word of a venerable ex-member can scarcely have much weight against the brilliancy of such still active adherents as may bark upon the other side. Aware of my ineptitude at argument, my valued correspondent Curator James Ferdinand Morton of Paterson has sent me the records of a similar controversy in the *New York Tribune,* in which Mr. Carl Van Doren is on my side and Mr. Albert Payson Terhune on that of the canine tribe.[*] From this I would be glad to plagiarise such data as I need; but Mr. Morton, with genuinely Machiavellian subtlety, has furnished me with only a part of the feline section whilst submitting the doggish brief in full. No doubt he imagines that this arrangement, in view of my own emphatic bias, makes for something like ultimate fairness; but for me it is exceedingly inconvenient, since it will force me to be more or less original in several parts of the ensuing remarks.

Between dogs and cats my degree of choice is so great that it would never occur to me to compare the two. I have no active dislike for dogs, any more than I have for monkeys,

---

[*] Carl Van Doren (1885–1950), American critic and biographer; Albert Payson Terhune (1872–1942), American novelist and the creator of Lassie. HPL expressed fondness for Terhune's stories in the *All-Story* in his letter to that magazine (7 March 1914). He also wrote a poem, "To Mr. Terhune, on His Historical Fiction." The discussion in the *New York Tribune* has not been located.

human beings, negroes, cows, sheep, or pterodactyls; but for the cat I have entertained a particular respect and affection ever since the earliest days of my infancy. In its flawless grace and superior self-sufficiency I have seen a symbol of the perfect beauty and bland impersonality of the universe itself, objectively considered; and in its air of silent mystery there resides for me all the wonder and fascination of the unknown. The dog appeals to cheap and facile emotions; the cat to the deepest founts of imagination and cosmic perception in the human mind. It is no accident that the contemplative Egyptians, together with such later poetic spirits as Poe, Gautier, Baudelaire, and Swinburne, were all sincere worshippers of the supple grimalkin.

Naturally, one's preference in the matter of cats and dogs depends wholly upon one's temperament and point of view. The dog would appear to me to be the favourite of superficial, sentimental, emotional, and democratic people—people who feel rather than think, who attach importance to mankind and the popular conventional emotions of the simple, and who find their greatest consolation in the fawning and dependent attachments of a gregarious society. Such people live in a limited world of imagination; accepting uncritically the values of common folklore, and always preferring to have their naive beliefs, feelings, and prejudices tickled, rather than to enjoy a purely aesthetic and philosophic pleasure arising from discrimination, contemplation, and the recognition of austere absolute beauty. This is not to say that the cheaper emotions do not also reside in the average cat-lover's love of cats, but merely to point out that in ailurophily there exists a basis of true aestheticism which kynophily does not possess. The real lover of cats is one who demands a clearer adjustment to the universe than ordinary household platitudes provide; one who refuses to swallow the sentimental notion that all good people love dogs, children, and horses while all bad people dislike and are disliked by such. He is unwilling to set up himself and his cruder feelings as a measure of universal values, or to allow shallow ethical notions to warp his judgment. In a word, he had rather admire and respect than effuse and dote; and does not fall into the fallacy that pointless sociability and friendliness, or slavering devotion and obedience, constitute anything intrinsically admirable or exalted. Dog-lovers base their whole case on these commonplace, servile, and plebeian qualities, and amusingly judge the intelligence of a pet by its degree of conformity to their own wishes. Cat-lovers escape this delusion, repudiate the idea that cringing subservience and sidling companionship to man are supreme merits, and stand free to worship aristocratic independence, self-respect, and individual personality joined to extreme grace and beauty as typified by the cool, lithe, cynical, and unconquered lord of the housetops.

Persons of commonplace ideas—unimaginative worthy burghers who are satisfied with the daily round of things and who subscribe to the popular credo of sentimental values—will always be dog-lovers. To them nothing will ever be more important than themselves and their own more primitive feelings, and they will never cease to esteem and glorify the fellow-animal who best typifies these. Such persons are submerged in the vortex of Oriental idealism and abasement which ruined classic civilisation in the Dark Ages,* and live in a bleak world of abstract sentimental values wherein the mawkish illusions of meekness, devotion, gentleness, brotherhood, and whining humility are magnified into supreme virtues, and a whole false ethic and philosophy erected on

---

* HPL refers to Christianity.

the timid reactions of the flexor system of muscles. This heritage, ironically foisted on us when Roman politics raised the faith of a whipped and broken people to supremacy in the later empire, has naturally kept a strong hold over the weak and the sentimentally thoughtless; and perhaps reached its culmination in the insipid nineteenth century, when people were wont to praise dogs "because they are so human" (as if humanity were any valid standard of merit!), and honest Edwin Landseer painted hundreds of smug Fidoes and Carlos and Rovers with all the anthropoid triviality, pettiness, and "cuteness" of eminent Victorians.[*]

But amidst this chaos of intellectual and emotional grovelling a few free souls have always stood out for the old civilised realities which mediaevalism eclipsed—the stern classic loyalty to truth, strength, and beauty given by a clear mind and uncowed spirit to the full-living Western Aryan confronted by Nature's majesty, loveliness, and aloofness. This is the virile aesthetic and ethic of the extensor muscles—the bold, buoyant, assertive beliefs and preferences of proud, dominant, unbroken, and unterrified conquerors, hunters, and warriors—and it has small use for the shams and whimperings of the brotherly, affection-slobbering peacemaker and cringer and sentimentalist. Beauty and sufficiency—twin qualities of the cosmos itself—are the gods of this aristocratic and pagan type; to the worshipper of such eternal things the supreme virtue will not be found in lowliness, attachment, obedience, and emotional messiness. This sort of worshipper will look for that which best embodies the loveliness of the stars and the worlds and the forests and the seas and the sun-

---

[*]Sir Edwin Henry Landseer (1802–1873), Scottish painter who specialised in the painting of Scottish landscapes as well as of dogs in natural settings. The phrase "eminent Victorians" is a nod to Lytton Strachey's cynical series of biographical portraits, *Eminent Victorians* (1918).

sets, and which best acts out the blandness, lordliness, accuracy, self-sufficiency, cruelty, independence, and contemptuous and capricious impersonality of all-governing Nature. Beauty—coolness—aloofness—philosophic repose—self-sufficiency—untamed mastery—where else can we find these things incarnated with even half the perfection and completeness that mark their incarnation in the peerless and softly gliding cat, which performs its mysterious orbit with the relentless and unobtrusive certainty of a planet in infinity?

That dogs are dear to the unimaginative peasant-burgher whilst cats appeal to the sensitive poet-aristocrat-philosopher will be clear in a moment when we reflect on the matter of biological association. Practical plebeian folk judge a thing only by its immediate touch, taste, and smell; while more delicate types form their estimates from the linked images and ideas which the object calls up in their minds. Now when dogs and cats are considered, the stolid churl sees only the two animals before him, and bases his favour on their relative capacity to pander to his sloppy, unformed ideas of ethics and friendship and flattering subservience. On the other hand the gentleman and thinker sees each in all its natural affiliations, and cannot fail to notice that in the great symmetries of organic life dogs fall in with slovenly wolves and foxes and jackals and coyotes and dingoes and painted hyaenas, whilst cats walk proudly with the jungle's lords, and own the haughty lion, the sinuous leopard, the regal tiger, and the shapely panther and jaguar as their kin. Dogs are the hieroglyphs of blind emotion, inferiority, servile attachment, and gregariousness—the attributes of commonplace, stupidly passionate, and intellectually and imaginatively undeveloped men. Cats are the runes of beauty, invincibility, wonder, pride, freedom, coldness, self-sufficiency, and dainty individuality—the qualities of sensitive, enlightened, mentally developed, pagan, cynical, poetic, philosophic, dispassionate, reserved, independent, Nietzschean, unbroken, civilised, master-class men. The dog is a peasant and the cat is a gentleman.

We may, indeed, judge the tone and bias of a civilisation by its relative attitude toward dogs and cats. The proud Egypt wherein Pharaoh was Pharaoh and pyramids rose in beauty at the wish of him who dreamed them bowed down to the cat, and temples were builded to its goddess at Bubastis. In imperial Rome the graceful leopard adorned most homes of quality, lounging in insolent beauty in the atrium with golden collar and chain; while after the age of the Antonines the actual cat was imported from Egypt and cherished as a rare and costly luxury. So much for dominant and enlightened peoples. When, however, we come to the grovelling Middle Ages with their superstitions and ecstasies and monasticisms and maunderings over saints and their relics, we find the cool and impersonal loveliness of the felidae in very low esteem; and behold a sorry spectacle of hatred and cruelty shewn toward the beautiful little creature whose mousing virtues alone gained it sufferance amongst the ignorant churls who resented its self-respecting coolness and feared its cryptical and elusive independence as something akin to the dark powers of witchcraft. These boorish slaves of eastern darkness could not tolerate what did not serve their own cheap emotions and flimsy purposes. They wished a dog to fawn and hunt and fetch and carry, and had no use for the cat's gift of eternal and disinterested beauty to feed the spirit. One can imagine how they must have resented Pussy's magnificent reposefulness, unhurriedness, relaxation, and scorn for trivial human aims and concernments. Throw a stick, and the servile dog wheezes and pants and shambles to bring it to you. Do the same before a cat, and he will eye you with coolly polite and somewhat bored amusement. And just as inferior people prefer the inferior animal which scampers excitedly because somebody else wants something, so do superior people respect the superior animal which lives its own life and knows that the puerile stick-throwings of alien bipeds are none of its business and beneath its notice. The dog barks and begs and tumbles to amuse you when you crack the whip. That pleases a meekness-loving peasant who relishes a stimulus to his sense of importance. The cat, on the other hand, charms you into playing for its benefit when it wishes to be amused; making you rush about the room with a paper on a string when it feels like exercise, but refusing all your attempts to make it play when it is not in the humour. That is personality and individuality and self-respect—the calm mastery of a being whose life is its own and not yours—and the superior person recognises and appreciates this because he too is a free soul whose position is assured, and whose only law is his own heritage and aesthetic sense. Altogether, we may see that the dog appeals to those primitive emotional souls whose chief demands on the universe are for meaningless affection, aimless companionship, and flattering attention and subservience; whilst the cat reigns among those more contemplative and imaginative spirits who ask of the universe only the objective sight of poignant, ethereal beauty and the animate symbolisation of Nature's bland, relentless, reposeful, unhurried, and impersonal order and sufficiency. The dog *gives,* but the cat *is.*

Simple folk always overstress the ethical element in life, and it is quite natural that they should extend it to the realm of their pets. Accordingly we hear many inane dicta in favour of dogs on the ground that they are *faithful,* whilst cats are *treacherous.* Now just what does this really mean? Where are the points of reference? Certainly, the dog has so little imagination and individuality that it knows no motives but its master's; but what sophisticated mind can descry a positive virtue in this stupid abnegation of a birthright? Discrimination must surely award the palm to the superior cat, which has too much natural dignity to accept any scheme of things but its own, and which consequently cares not one whit what any clumsy human thinks or wishes or expects of it. It is not *treacherous,* because it has never acknowledged any allegiance to anything outside its own leisurely wishes; and *treachery* basically implies a departure from some covenant explicitly recognised. The cat is a realist, and no hypocrite. He takes what pleases him when he wants it, and makes no promises. He never leads you to expect more from him than he gives, and if you choose to be stupidly Victorian enough to mistake his purrs and rubbings of self-satisfaction for marks of transient affection toward you, that is no fault of his. He would not for a moment have you believe that he wants more of you than food and warmth and shelter and amusement—and he is certainly justified in criticising your aesthetic and imaginative development if you fail to find his grace, beauty, and cheerful decorative influence an aboundingly sufficient repayment for all that you give him. The cat-lover need not be amazed at another's love for dogs—indeed, he may also possess this quality himself; for dogs are often very comely, and as lovable in a condescending way as a faithful old servant or tenant in the eyes of a master—but he cannot help feeling astonishment at those who do not share his love for cats. The cat is such a perfect symbol of beauty and superiority that it seems scarcely possible for any true aesthete and civilised cynic to do other than worship it. We call ourselves a dog's "master"—but who ever dared to call himself the "master" of a cat? We *own* a dog—he is with us as a slave and inferior because we wish him to be. But we *entertain* a cat—he adorns our hearth as a guest, fellow-lodger, and equal because *he* wishes to be there. It is no compliment to be the stupidly idolised master of a dog whose instinct it is to idolise, but it is a very distinct tribute to be chosen as the friend and confidant of a philosophic cat who is wholly his own master and could easily choose another companion if he found such an one more agreeable and interesting. A trace, I think, of this great truth regarding the higher dignity of the cat has crept into folklore in the use of the names "cat" and "dog" as terms of opprobrium. Whilst "cat" has never been applied to any sort of offender more serious than the mildly spiteful and innocuously sly female gossip and commentator, the words "dog" and "cur" have always been linked with vileness, dishonour, and degradation of the gravest type. In the crystallisation of this nomenclature there has undoubtedly been present in the popular mind some dim, half-unconscious realisation that there are depths of slinking, whining, fawning, and servile ignobility which no kith of the lion and the leopard could ever attain. The cat may fall low, but he is always unbroken. He is, like the Nordic among men, one of those who govern their own lives or die.

We have but to glance analytically at the two animals to see the points pile up in favour of the cat. Beauty, which is probably the only thing of any basic significance in all the cosmos, ought to be our chief criterion; and here the cat excels so brilliantly that all comparisons collapse. Some dogs, it is true, have beauty in a very ample degree; but even the highest level of canine beauty falls far below the feline average. The cat is classic whilst the dog is Gothic—nowhere in the animal world can we discover such really Hellenic perfection of form, with anatomy adapted to function, as in the felidae.

Puss is a Doric temple—an Ionic colonnade—in the utter classicism of its structural and decorative harmonies. And this is just as true kinetically as statically, for art has no parallel for the bewitching grace of the cat's slightest motion. The sheer, perfect aestheticism of kitty's lazy stretchings, industrious face-washings, playful rollings, and little involuntary shiftings in sleep is something as keen and vital as the best pastoral poetry or genre painting; whilst the unerring accuracy of his leaping and springing, running and hunting, has an art-value just as high in a more spirited way. But it is his capacity for leisure and repose which makes the cat preëminent. Mr. Carl Van Vechten, in "Peter Whiffle",[*] holds up the timeless restfulness of the cat as a model for a life's philosophy, and Prof. William Lyon Phelps has very effectively captured the secret of felinity when he says that the cat does not merely *lie down,* but *"pours his body out on the floor like a glass of water".*[**] What other creature has thus merged the aestheticism of mechanics and hydraulics? Contrast with this the inept panting, wheezing, fumbling, drooling, scratching, and general clumsiness of the average dog with his myriad false and wasted motions. And in the detail of neatness the fastidious cat is of course immeasurably ahead. We always love to touch a cat, but only the insensitive can uniformly welcome the frantic and humid nuzzlings and pawings of a dusty and perhaps not inodorous canine which leaps and fusses and writhes about in awkward feverishness for no particular reason save that blind nerve-centres have been spurred by certain meaningless stimuli. There is a wearying excess of bad

[*] See Carl Van Vechten (1880–1964), *Peter Whiffle* (1922), ch. 9. Van Vechten also wrote an entire book about cats, *The Tiger in the House* (1920).

[**] William Lyon Phelps (1865–1943), American critic and professor of English at Yale from 1892 to 1933. The quotation is from his "As I Like It" column in *Scribner's Magazine* 75, No. 1 (January 1924): 117. The entire column is about cats.

manners in all this doggish fury—well-bred people don't paw and maul one, and surely enough we invariably find the cat gentle and reserved in his advances, and delicate even when he glides gracefully into your lap with cultivated purrs, or leaps whimsically on the table where you are writing to play with your pen in modulated, serio-comic pats. I do not wonder that Mahomet, that sheik of perfect manners, loved cats for their urbanity and disliked dogs for their boorishness; or that cats are the favourites in the polite Latin countries whilst dogs take the lead in heavy, practical, and beer-drinking Central Europe. Watch a cat eat, and then watch a dog. The one is held in check by an inherent and inescapable daintiness, and lends a kind of grace to one of the most ungraceful of all processes. The dog, on the other hand, is wholly repulsive in his bestial and insatiate greediness; living up to his forest kinship by "wolfing" most openly and unashamedly. Returning to beauty of line—is it not significant that while many normal breeds of dogs are conspicuously and admittedly ugly, *no* healthy and well-developed feline of any species whatsoever is other than beautiful? There are, of course, many ugly cats; but these are always individual cases of mongrelism, malnutrition, deformity, or injury. No breed of cats in its proper condition can by any stretch of the imagination be thought of as even slightly ungraceful—a record against which must be pitted the depressing spectacle of impossibly flattened bulldogs, grotesquely elongated dachshunds, hideously shapeless and shaggy Airedales, and the like. Of course, it may be said that no aesthetic standard is other than relative—but we always work with such standards as we empirically have, and in comparing cats and dogs under the Western European aesthetic we cannot be unfair to either. If any undiscovered tribe in Thibet finds Airedales beautiful and Persian cats ugly, we will not dispute them on their own territory—but just now we are dealing with ourselves and our territory, and here the verdict would not admit of much doubt even from the most ardent kynophile. Such an one usually passes the problem off in an epigrammatic paradox, and says 'that Snookums is so homely, he's pretty!' This is the childish penchant for the grotesque and tawdrily 'cute', which we see likewise embodied in popular cartoons, freak dolls, and all the malformed decorative trumpery of the "Billiken" or "Krazy Kat"* order found in the "dens" and "cosy corners" of the would-be sophisticated cultural yokelry.

In the matter of intelligence we find the caninites making amusing claims—amusing because they so naively measure what they conceive to be an animal's intelligence by its degree of subservience to the human will. A dog will retrieve, a cat will not; *therefore* (sic!) the dog is the more intelligent. Dogs can be more elaborately trained for circus and vaudeville acts than cats, *therefore* (O Zeus, O Royal Mount!) they are cerebrally superior. Now of course this is all the sheerest nonsense. We would not call a weak-spirited man more intelligent than an independent citizen because we can make him vote as we wish whereas we can't influence the independent citizen, yet countless persons apply an exactly parallel argument in appraising the grey matter of dogs and cats. Competition in servility is something to which no self-respecting Thomas or Tabitha ever stooped, and it is plain that any really effective estimate of canine and feline intelligence must proceed from a careful observation of dogs and cats in a detached state—uninfluenced by human beings—as they formulate certain objectives of their own and use their own mental equipment in

* "Billiken" refers to a series of dolls manufactured by the E. I. Horsman Company beginning in 1909. "Krazy Kat" was a popular comic strip of the 1910s and 1920s written by George Herriman (1880–1944).

achieving them. When we do this, we arrive at a very wholesome respect for our purring hearthside friend who makes so little display and ado about his wishes and business methods; for in every conception and calculation he shews a steel-cold and deliberate union of intellect, will, and sense of proportion which puts utterly to shame the emotional sloppings-over and docilely acquired artificial tricks of the "clever" and "faithful" pointer or sheep-dog. Watch a cat decide to move through a door, and see how patiently he waits for his opportunity, never losing sight of his purpose even when he finds it expedient to feign other interests in the interim. Watch him in the thick of the chase, and compare his calculating patience and quiet study of his terrain with the noisy floundering and pawing of his canine rival. It is not often that he returns empty-handed. He knows what he wants, and means to get it in the most effective way, even at the sacrifice of time—which he philosophically recognises as unimportant in the aimless cosmos. There is no turning him aside or distracting his attention—and we know that among humans this very quality of mental tenacity, this ability to carry a single thread through complex distractions, is considered a pretty good sign of intellectual vigour and maturity. Children, old crones, peasants, and dogs ramble; cats and philosophers stick to their point. In resourcefulness, too, the cat attests his superiority. Dogs can be well trained to do a single thing, but psychologists tell us that these responses to an automatic memory instilled from outside are of little worth as indices of real intelligence. To judge the abstract development of a brain, confront it with new and unfamiliar conditions and see how well its own strength enables it to achieve its object by sheer reasoning without blazed trails. Here the cat can silently devise a dozen mysterious and successful alternatives whilst poor Fido is barking in bewilderment and wondering what it is all about. Granted that Rover the retriever may make a greater bid for popular sentimental regard by going into the burning house and saving the baby in traditional cinema fashion, it remains a fact that whiskered and purring Nig is a higher-grade biological organism—something physiologically and psychologically nearer a man because of his very freedom from man's orders, and as such entitled to a higher respect from those who judge by purely philosophic and aesthetic standards. We can respect a cat as we cannot respect a dog, no matter which personally appeals the more to our mere doting fancy; and if we be aesthetes and analysts rather than commonplace-lovers and emotionalists, the scales must inevitably turn completely in kitty's favour. It may be added, moreover, that even the aloof and sufficient cat is by no means devoid of sentimental appeal. Once we get rid of the uncivilised ethical bias—the 'treacherous' and 'horrid bird-catcher' prejudice—we find in the 'harmless, necessary cat'* the very apex of happy domestic symbolism; whilst small kittens become objects to adore, idealise, and celebrate in the most rhapsodic of dactyls and anapaests, iambics and trochaics. I, in my own senescent mellowness, confess to an inordinate and wholly unphilosophic predilection for tiny coal-black kitties with large yellow eyes, and could no more pass one without petting him than Dr. Johnson could pass a sidewalk post without striking it. There is, likewise, in many cats something quite analogous to the reciprocal fondness so loudly extolled in dogs, human beings, horses, and the like. Cats come to associate certain persons with acts continuously contributing to their pleasure, and acquire for them a recognition and attachment which manifests itself in pleasant excitement at their approach—whether

---

* Shakespeare, *The Merchant of Venice* 4.1.55.

or not bearing food and drink—and a certain pensiveness at their protracted absence. The late "Tat" of Allston and Malden, grey companion of our fellow-amateur Mrs. Miniter, reached the point of accepting food from no other hand but hers, and would actually go hungry rather than touch the least morsel from a kindly Parker source.** He also had distinct affections amongst the other cats of that idyllic household; voluntarily offering food to one of his whiskered friends, whilst disputing most savagely the least glance which his coal-black rival "Snowball" would bestow upon his plate. If it be argued that these feline fondnesses are essentially 'selfish' and 'practical' in their ultimate composition, let us inquire in return how many human fondnesses, apart from those springing directly upon primitive brute instinct, have any other basis. After the returning board has brought in the grand total of zero we shall be better able to refrain from ingenuous censure of the 'selfish' cat.

The superior imaginative inner life of the cat, resulting in superior self-possession, is well known. A dog is a pitiful thing, depending wholly on companionship, and utterly lost except in packs or by the side of his master. Leave him alone and he does not know what to do except bark and howl and trot about till sheer exhaustion forces him to sleep. A cat, however, is never without the potentialities of contentment. Like a superior man, he knows how to be alone and happy. Once he looks about and finds no one to amuse him, he settles down to the task of amusing himself; and no one really knows cats without having occasionally peeked stealthily at

---

** A cat owned by Edith Miniter, who resided successively in Allston and Malden, Mass. HPL visited her in these residences in 1920–21 and later wrote a series of poems, "Veteropinguis Redivivus," commemorating her numerous cats and dogs (although there is no poem about Tat). "Parker" refers to the amateur writer and publisher Charles A. A. Parker, who resided with Miniter.

some lively and well-balanced kitten which believes itself to be alone. Only after such a glimpse of unaffected tail-chasing grace and unstudied purring can one fully understand the charm of those lines which Coleridge wrote with reference to the human rather than the feline young

> "... a limber elf,
> Singing, dancing to itself."[*]

But whole volumes could be written on the playing of cats, since the varieties and aesthetic aspects of such sportiveness are infinite. Be it sufficient to say that in such pastimes many cats have exhibited traits and actions which psychologists authentically declare to be motivated by genuine humour and whimsicality in its purest sense; so that the task of 'making a cat laugh' may not be so impossible a thing even outside the borders of Cheshire. In short, a dog is an incomplete thing. Like an inferior man, he needs emotional stimuli from outside, and must set something artificial up as a god and motive. The cat, however, is perfect in himself. Like the human philosopher, he is a self-sufficient entity and microcosm. He is a real and integrated being because he thinks and feels himself to be such, whereas the dog can conceive of himself only in relation to something else. Whip a dog and he licks your hand—faugh! The beast has no idea of himself except as an inferior part of an organism whereof you are a superior part—he would no more think of striking back at you than you would think of pounding your own head when it punishes you with a headache. But whip a cat and watch it glare and move backward hissing in outraged dignity and self-respect! One more blow, and it strikes you in return; for

---

[*] Samuel Taylor Coleridge (1772–1834), *Christabel* (1797–1801), ll. 656–57.

it is a gentleman and your equal, and will accept no infringement on its personality and body of privileges. It is only in your house anyway because it wishes to be, or perhaps even as a condescending favour to yourself. It is the house, not you, it likes; for philosophers realise that human beings are at best only minor adjuncts to scenery. Go one step too far, and it leaves you altogether. You have mistaken your relationship to it and imagined you are its master, and no real cat can tolerate that breach of good manners. Henceforward it will seek companions of greater discrimination and clearer perspective. Let anaemic persons who believe in 'turning the other cheek' console themselves with cringing dogs—for the robust pagan with the blood of Nordic twilights in his veins there is no beast like the cat; intrepid steed of Freya, who can boldly look even Thor and Odin full in the face and stare contemplatively with great round eyes of undimmed yellow or green.

And so, Sir (I employ the singular since I cannot imagine that you, O Jacobe Ferdinande, would have the truly feline cruelty to spring all these ten-plus pages on a deserving club which has never done you any harm), I believe I have outlined for you with some fulness the divers reasons why, in my opinion and in the smartly timed title-phrase of Mr. Van Doren, "gentlemen prefer cats". The reply of Mr. Terhune in a subsequent issue of the *Tribune* appears to me beside the point; insomuch as it is less a refutation of facts than a mere personal affirmation of the author's membership in that conventional "very human" majority who take affection and companionship seriously, enjoy being important to something alive, measure merit by devotion to human purposes, hate a "parasite" on mere ethical grounds without consulting the right of beauty to exist for its own sake, and therefore love man's noblest and most faithful friend, the perennial dog. I suppose Mr. Terhune loves horses and babies also, for they go conventionally together in the great hundred-per-center's credo as highly essential likings for every good and lovable he-man of the Arrow Collar and Harold Bell Wright[*] hero school, even though the motor car and dear Mrs. Sanger[**] have done much to reduce the last two items.

Dogs, then, are peasants and the pets of peasants; cats are gentlemen and the pets of gentlemen. The dog is for him who places crude feeling and outgrown ethics and humano-centricity above austere and disinterested beauty; who just loves 'folks and folksiness' and doesn't mind sloppy clumsiness if only something will truly care for him. (Tableau of dog across master's grave—cf. Landseer, "The Old Shepherd's Chief Mourner".) The guy who isn't much for highbrow stuff, but is always on the square and don't (sic) often find the Saddypost or the N.Y. World too deep for him; who hadn't much use for Valentino, but thinks Doug Fairbanks is just about right for an evening's entertainment. Wholesome—constructive—non-morbid—civic-minded—domestic—(I forgot to mention the radio) normal—that's the sort of go-getter that had ought to go in for dogs.

The cat is for the aristocrat—whether by birth or inclinations or both—who admires his fellow-aristocrats (even if Little Belknap isn't especially fond of Felis).[***] He is for the man who appreciates beauty as the one living force in a blind and purposeless universe, and who worships that beauty in all its forms without regard for the sentimental and ethical illusions of the moment. For the man who knows the hollowness of

[*] Harold Bell Wright (1872–1944), best-selling American novelist whom HPL regarded as a prototypical hack writer.

[**] Margaret Sanger (1883–1966), American pioneer of birth control.

[***] For Frank Belknap Long's haughty cat Felis, see his prose-poem "Felis" (printed in the Appendix).

feeling and the emptiness of human objects and aspirations, and who therefore clings solely to what is real—as beauty is real because it pretends to no significance beyond the emotion which it excites and is. For the man who feels sufficient in the cosmos, and asks no false perspective of exaltation; who is moved by no mawkish scruples of conventional prejudice, but loves repose and strength and freedom and luxury and superiority and sufficiency and contemplation; who as a strong fearless soul wishes something to respect instead of something to lick his face and accept his alternate blows and strokings; who seeks a proud and beautiful equal in the peerage of individualism rather than a cowed and cringing satellite in the hierarchy of fear, subservience, and devotion. The cat is not for the brisk, self-important little worker with a "mission", but for the enlightened dreaming poet who knows that the world contains nothing really worth doing. The dilettante—the connoisseur—the decadent, if you will, though in a healthier age than this there were things for such men to do, so that they were the planners and leaders of those glorious pagan times. The cat is for him who does things not for empty duty but for power, pleasure, splendour, romance, and glamour—for the harpist who sings alone in the night of old battles, or the warrior who goes out to fight such battles for beauty, glory, fame, and the splendour of a kingly court athwart which no shadow of weakness or democracy falls. For him who will be lulled by no sops of prose and usefulness, but demands for his effort the ease and beauty and ascendancy and cultivation which alone make effort worth while. For the man who knows that play, not work, and leisure, not bustle, are the great things of life; and that the round of striving merely in order to strive some more is a bitter irony of which the civilised soul accepts as little as it can.

Beauty, sufficiency, ease, and good manners—what more can civilisation require? We have them all in the divine little monarch who lounges gloriously on his silken cushion before the hearth. Loveliness and joy for their own sake—pride and harmony and coördination—spirit, restfulness, and completeness—all here are present, and need but a sympathetic disillusionment for worship in full measure. What fully civilised soul but would eagerly serve as high-priest of Bast? The star of the cat, I think, is just now in the ascendant, as we emerge little by little from the dreams of ethics and democracy which clouded the nineteenth century and raised the grubbing and unlovely dog to the pinnacle of sentimental regard. Whether a renaissance of monarchy and beauty will restore our Western civilisation, or whether the forces of disintegration are already too powerful for even the fascist sentiment to check, none may yet say; but in the present moment of cynical world-unmasking between the pretence of the eighteen-hundreds and the ominous mystery of the decades ahead we have at least a flash of the old pagan perspective and the old pagan clearness and honesty.

And one idol lit up by that flash, seen fair and lovely on a dream-throne of silk and gold under a chryselephantine dome, is a shape of deathless grace not always given its due among groping mortals—the haughty, the unconquered, the mysterious, the luxurious, the Babylonian, the impersonal, the eternal companion of superiority and art—the type of perfect beauty and the brother of poetry—the bland, grave, competent, and patrician cat.

The Dream-Quest of Unknown Kadath

When the galley landed at a greasy-looking quay of spongy rock a nightmare horde of toad-things wriggled out of the hatches, and two of them seized Carter and dragged him ashore. The smell and aspect of that city are beyond telling, and Carter held only scattered images of the tiled streets and black doorways and endless precipices of grey vertical walls without windows. At length he was dragged within a low doorway and made to climb infinite steps in pitch blackness. It was, apparently, all one to the toad-things whether it were light or dark. The odour of the place was intolerable, and when Carter was locked into a chamber and left alone he scarcely had strength to crawl around and ascertain its form and dimensions. It was circular, and about twenty feet across.

From then on time ceased to exist. At intervals food was pushed in, but Carter would not touch it. What his fate would be, he did not know; but he felt that he was held for the coming of that frightful soul and messenger of infinity's Other Gods, the crawling chaos Nyarlathotep. Finally, after an unguessed span of hours or days, the great stone door swung wide again and Carter was shoved down the stairs and out into the red-litten streets of that fearsome city. It was night on the moon, and all through the town were stationed slaves bearing torches.

In a destestable square a sort of procession was formed; ten of the toad-things and twenty-four almost-human torch-bearers, eleven on either side, and one each before and behind. Carter was placed in the middle of the line; five toad-things ahead and five behind, and one almost-human torch-bearer on each side of him. Certain of the toad-things produced disgustingly carven flutes of ivory and made loathsome sounds. To that hellish piping the column advanced out of the tiled streets and into nighted plains of obscene fungi, soon commencing to climb one of the lower and more gradual hills that lay behind the city. That on some frightful slope or blasphemous plateau the crawling chaos waited, Carter could not doubt; and he wished that the suspense might soon be over. The whining of those impious flutes was shocking, and he would have given worlds for some even half-normal sound; but these toad-things had no voices, and the slaves did not talk.

Then through that star-specked darkness there did come a normal sound. It rolled from the higher hills, and from all the jagged peaks around it was caught up and echoed in a swelling pandaemoniac chorus. It was the mignight yell of the cat, and Carter knew at last that the old village folk were right when they made low guesses about the cryptical realms which are known only to cats, and to which the elders among cats repair by stealth nocturnally, springing from high housetops. Verily, it is to the moon's dark side that they go to leap and gambol on the hills and converse with ancient shadows, and here amidst that column of foetid things Carter heard their homely, friendly cry, and thought of the steep roofs and warm hearths and little lighted windows of home.

Now much of the speech of cats was known to Randolph Carter, and in this far, terrible place he uttered the cry that was suitable. But that he need not have done, for even as his lips opened he heard the chorus wax and draw nearer, and saw swift shadows against the stars as small graceful shapes leaped from hill to hill in gathering legions. The call of the clan had been given, and before the foul procession had time even to be frightened a cloud of smothering fur and a phalanx of murderous claws were tidally and tempestuously upon it. The flutes stopped, and there were shrieks in the night. Dying almost-humans screamed, and cats spit and yowled and roared, but the toad-things made never a sound as their stinking green ichor oozed fatally upon that porous earth with the obscene fungi.

It was a stupendous sight while the torches lasted, and Carter had never before seen so many cats. Black, grey, and white; yellow, tiger, and mixed; common, Persian, and Manx; Thibetan, Angora, and Egyptian; all were there in the fury of battle, and there hovered over them some trace of that profound and inviolate sanctity which made their goddess great in the temples of Bubastis. They would leap seven strong at the throat of an almost-human or the pink tentacled snout of a toad-thing and drag it down savagely to the fungous plain, where myriads of their fellows would surge over it and into it with the frenzied claws and teeth of a divine battle-fury. Carter had seized a torch from a stricken slave, but was soon overborne by the surging waves of his loyal defenders. Then he lay in the utter blackness hearing the clangour of war and the shouts of the victors, and feeling the soft paws of his friends as they rushed to and fro over him in the fray.

At last awe and exhaustion closed his eyes, and when he opened them again it was upon a strange scene. The great shining disc of the earth, thirteen times greater than that of the moon as we see it, had risen with floods of weird light over the lunar landscape; and across all those leagues of wild plateau and ragged crest there squatted one endless sea of cats in orderly array. Circle on circle they reached, and two or three leaders out of the ranks were licking his face and purring to him consolingly. Of the dead slaves and toad-things there were not many signs, but Carter thought he saw one bone a little way off in the open space between him and the beginning of the solid circles of the warriors.

Carter now spoke with the leaders in the soft language of cats, and learned that his ancient friendship with the species was well known and often spoken of in the places where cats congregate. He had not been unmarked in Ulthar when he passed through, and the sleek old cats had remembered how he petted them after they had attended to the hungry zoogs who looked evilly at a small black kitten. And they recalled, too, how he had welcomed the very little kitten who came to see him at the inn, and how he had given it a saucer of rich cream in the morning before he left. The grandfather of that very little kitten was the leader of the army now assembled, for he had seen the evil procession from a far hill and recognised the prisoner as a sworn friend of his kind on earth and in the land of dream.

A yowl now came from a farther peak, and the old leader paused abruptly in his conversation. It was one of the army's outposts, stationed on the highest of the mountains to watch the one foe which earth's cats fear; the very large and peculiar cats from Saturn, who for some reason have not been oblivious of the charm of our moon's dark side. They are leagued by treaty with the evil toad-things, and are notoriously hostile to our earthly cats; so that at this juncture a meeting would have been a somewhat grave matter.

After a brief consultation of generals, the cats rose and assumed a closer formation, crowding protectingly around Carter and preparing to take the great leap through space back to the housetops of our earth and its dreamland. The old field-marshal advised Carter to let himself be borne along

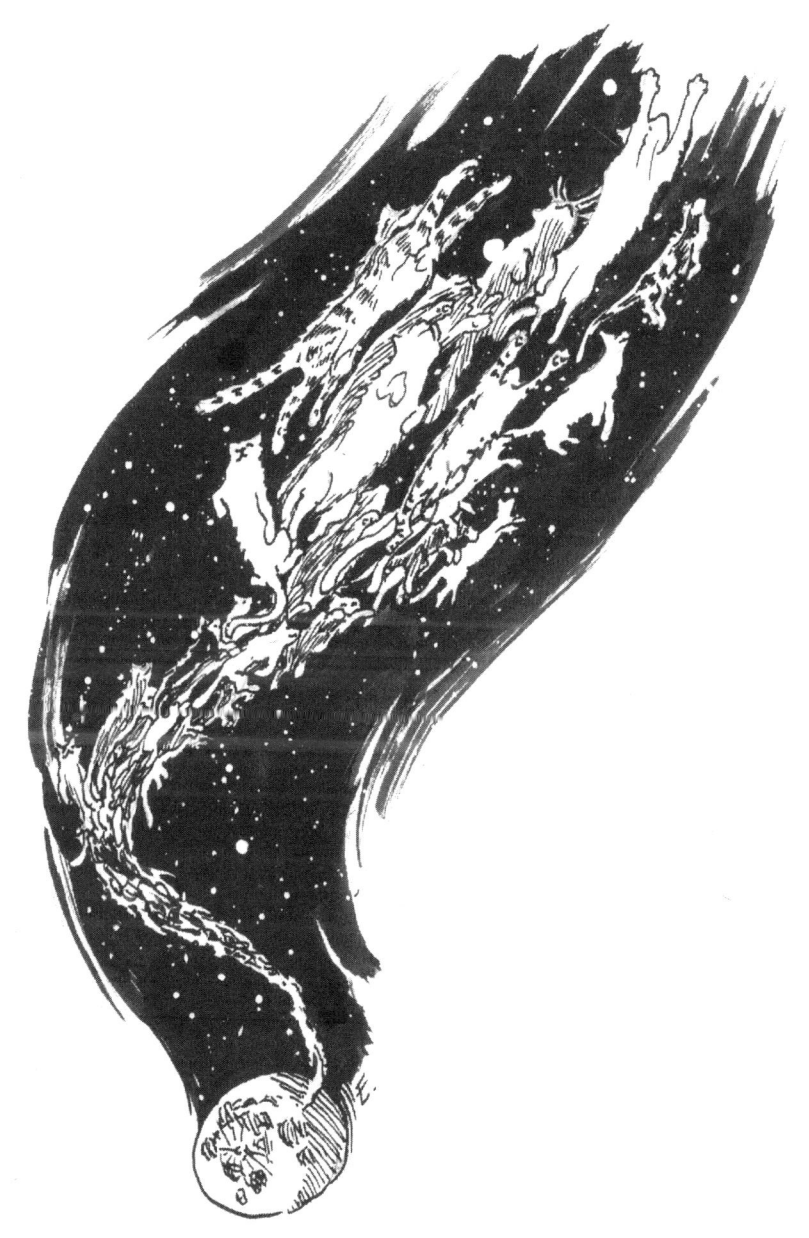

smoothly and passively in the massed ranks of furry leapers, and told him how to spring when the rest sprang and land gracefully when the rest landed. He also offered to deposit him in any spot he desired, and Carter decided on the city of Dylath-Leen whence the black galley had set out; for he wished to sail thence for Oriab and the carven crest of Ngranek, and also to warn the people of the city to have no more traffick with black galleys, if indeed that traffick could be tactfully and judiciously broken off. Then, upon a signal, the cats all leaped gracefully with their friend packed securely in their midst; while in a black cave on a far unhallowed summit of the moon-mountains still vainly waited the crawling chaos Nyarlathotep.

The leap of the cats through space was very swift; and being surrounded by his companions, Carter did not see this time the great black shapelessnesses that lurk and caper and flounder in the abyss. Before he fully realised what had happened he was back in his familiar room at the inn at Dylath-Leen, and the stealthy, friendly cats were pouring out of the window in streams. The old leader from Ulthar was the last to leave, and as Carter shook his paw he said he would be able to get home by cockcrow. When dawn came, Carter went downstairs and learned that a week had elapsed since his capture and leaving. There was still nearly a fortnight to wait for the ship bound toward Oriab, and during that time he said what he could against the black galleys and their infamous ways. Most of the townsfolk believed him; yet so fond were the jewellers of great rubies that none would wholly promise to cease trafficking with the wide-mouthed merchants. If aught of evil ever befalls Dylath-Leen through such traffick, it will not be his fault.

Veteropinguis Redivivus

1. *Veteropinguis Redivivus: A Poem*
Let the sad cypress and the yew
'Neath bays and myrtle sink from view,
      And to oblivion fly;
For lying Rumour's pow'r is riv'n,
As from a mythic grave is giv'n
      A form too tough to die.

An ear or nose, by Nature's law,
The fates of warfare well may chaw;
      What oak's too strong to bend?
But not so easy does the fire
Of ninefold feline life expire,
      And in dull embers end!

Hail to the rustick batter'd form
That stoutly weathers ev'ry storm
      And howls triumphant still!
Tho' yet unskill'd in elder ways,
And alien to the chimney's maze,
      Thou spurnst the clutch of ill!

Long may the placid twelvemonths glide
With thee a-trotting by our side,
    Terror of neighb'ring rats!
May Time preserve thee hale and old,
Thy fur and heart alike of gold—
    Dean of the Pack—Old Fats!

2.
Our sadden'd orbs o'erflow with pensive brine,
    And linger on the vacant hearthside space,
For gentle Pettie, seiz'd with a decline,
    Will nevermore display his polisht grace.

That golden soul, too delicate for earth,
    Mourn'd for old Printer's counsel, calm and wise;
And sick'ning at the unaccustom'd dearth,
    Follow'd his lov'd preceptor to the skies.

3.
Underneath this ferreous bowl
Lyes the matron we extol;
Pettie's sister, Marcelle's mother.
Death, ere thou hast kill'd another
Wise and good as this lost kit,
Time will pause a Little Bit.

4.
Donald, since last you met my aged eyes
It seems you have increas'd somewhat in size:
What alien sire can thus have summon'd up
A tow'ring monster from a sportive pup?

Once I'd have said, a china-shatt'ring Taurus—
But now, I swear it was a brontosaurus!

5.
A health to the train that unflagging uphold
The traditions bequeath'd by Bubastis of old:
Old Fats—in whose roughness lies many a charm;
And the Prince whose proud ermine no clawing can harm;
Lithe Tardee, the scourge of each mouse-hole and glade;
Marcelle, whom a thousand bold Toms serenade;
And last but not hindmost there floats on the tide
Light, oöphagous Corky, the future's young pride!

6.
To this calm spot where many a slab and urn
        Attests the shortness of our mortal span,
For pensive meditation I return,
        Pond'ring the woes of Heav'n's terrestrial plan.

On ev'ry hand memorial blossoms bloom,
        But sadder than the saddest of them all
Is one press'd petal from a distant tomb,
        That can old PRINTER'S lov'd grey form recall.

7.
STITCHIE, tho' eye and ear
        For you be going under,
May this but keep you clear
        Of vexing flash and thunder!

With worth that flouts decay,
        Tho' sight and sound be jaded,
You face the close of day—

A gentleman unfaded!

8.
Suspitious Souls with Pride are wont to tell
How quick they can a Rodent's Presence smell;
Yet if the scamp'ring Train be swift and small,
'Tis easie not to glimpse the Rogues at all.
In PRINTER's Day, when Act was quick as Thought,
How few the Mice that cou'd survive uncaught!
Our languid Age displays a lesser Skill,
And the brown Nibblers vex our Cheese at will!
But here and there, where western Rivers pour,
Young Heads preserve their Sires' forgotten Lore;
Catch the old Scent, and trap for future Time
The brood that burrows deep in doubtful Rhyme.

[To a Cat]

Last of an elder race, whose treasur'd lore
    No younger hierophant deserv'd to share!
May Fortune grant thee, on a sunnier shore,
    Eternal hours exempt from worldly care.

May heav'nly ladders bear thee from this earth,
    Up hidden flues to realms of endless day,
Where bliss shall crown thy time-attested worth
    In fields of catnip rich with rodent prey.

[Little Sam Perkins]

The ancient garden seems tonight
    A deeper gloom to bear,
As if some silent shadow's blight
    Were hov'ring in the air.

With hidden griefs the grasses sway,
    Unable quite to word them—
Remembering from yesterday
    The little paws that stirr'd them.

[Christmas Greetings]

[To Tat (Edith Miniter's cat)]

As once *Hortensia*, mythical and bright,
A sparkish COLE to couplets could incite;
So thou, Sir *Tatt*, with less fictitious grace,
Inspir'st a lover of thy furry race!

[To Felis (Frank Belknap Long's cat)]

Little Tiger, burning bright
With a subtle Blakeish light,
Tell what visions have their home
In those eyes of flame and chrome!
Children vex thee—thoughtless, gay—
Holding when thou wouldst away:
What dark lore is that which thou,
Spitting, mixest with thy meow?

[To Tat (Edith Miniter's cat)]

Tom Grey, 'tis no elegiack strain
        I sound in Yuletide gratulation,
For sure, I hope it still is plain
        Your state is one of animation.

As far from my Novanglian lea
        I meditate in many a boneyard,
The grey slabs turn my thoughts to thee,
        Yet purring gravely in thine own yard.

[To a cat]

With catnip deck the temple doors,
          And to the gods a fat mouse offer—
Tonight our annual praise outpours
          In pious purrs that mock the scoffer.
Let not a claw disturb the bliss,
          Let not a back in scorn be vaulted.
Lives there a cat with sceptick hiss
          Or meow for worship so exalted?

[To Felis (Frank Belknap Long's cat)]

Haughty Sphinx, whose amber eyes
Hold the secrets of the skies,
As thou ripplest in thy grace,
Round the chairs and chimney-place,
Scorn on thy patrician face:
Hiss not harsh, nor use thy claws
On the hand that gives applause—
Good-will only doth abide
In these lines at Christmastide!

The Cats of New York City and Environs

Yesterday Morton & I went over to Long's—the kid is just back from Atlantic City—& had a marvellous afternoon of literary & philosophical debate. Felis, the kid's glossy & ornate coon cat, sat purring in my lap whilst Democritus, Epicurus, Aristippus, Lucretius, Plato, Aristotle, & other sages filled the air.

—To Annie E. P. Gamwell, 9–11 September 1922

[. . .] you cannot fail to be captivated by little Belknap's marvellous coon cat, "Felis"—one of the most artistic & intellectual persons of his kind whom I have ever met.

—To Annie E. P. Gamwell, 24 September 1922

About the premises [of the Dyckman Cottage] was the most attractive *black cat* conceivable. I held him during most of my stay, & he assured me that he is descended from the very best cats of Amsterdam, his family having been purely Dutch except for one ancestor, Tomas Le Chat, who came from Brussells [sic] in 1596 & is said to have been the grandson of a noted cat of Paris.

—To Lillian D. Clark, 29 September 1922

On the corner of Washington-Square and McDougall-Street, in the iron-fenc'd yard of a colonial mansion, we beheld a fine plump black-and-white cat. A moment later another appear'd—this one jet black, like my old nigger-man. In two more moments a prepossessing tiger join'd the company; and

by the time I had stoop'd to stroke the haughty blackamoor, no less than six or seven had assembled; some friendly, some indifferent, and some frankly curious. It was a feline convention; and, Khatist that I am, I made the most of it in purring and intelligent conversation. In vain did my spouse seek to set me in motion . . . . should not an old tomcat occasionally pause to chat with the furry cronies of his youth? Finally, though, when I had sighted another cat—a black and yellow aristocrat perched on the outside of an ancient small-paned window—and was about to begin a fresh discussion with him, S.H. dragg'd me away by main force; checking resistance by pointing to counter-attractions ahead . . . . . Colonial gables and distant Georgian chimney-pots in West Fourth Street.
—*To Lillian D. Clark, 20 August 1924*

After this we fared westward to the elevated, where after a bit of lunch—the third that evening, counting some coffee previously absorbed in Sheridan Square—we took the elevated for lower Manhattan. On the ride we digested what we had seen, and Samuelus opined what he afterward reiterated, that one of the quaintest features of all colonial New York is the number of cats seen at large. There was a charming maltese kitten in Minetta Place which I could hardly resist taking home in my pocket!
—*To Lillian D. Clark, 29–30 September 1924*

From the Van Cortlandt [house] we rode down to the Dyckman, where we repeated our experience & ecstasy. An added joy for me was a little grey-&-white kittie—a real Dutch Dyckman kittie—who purred contentedly in my arms during the entire tour of the place. You will recall that when I explored this house two years ago, I held a black cat, & fell down the cellar stairs with him. This time I didn't fall—though I stove in my hat (fortunately soft felt) against the low rafters on that same staircase!!

—*To Lillian D. Clark, 4–6 November 1924*

Our journey was accomplished without incident—across to Jersey City & by train to Somerville—& we were met at the station by the eldest son of the hostess—Mrs. R. A. Craig—in a battered Chevrolet car. [. . .] There are at least *seven cats.* Two adults, (maltese & tiger) two half-grown & delectably pugilistic kittens, (one yellow & one maltese) & three very little kittens—captivating handfuls of tender grey fuzziness with beautiful faces & great saucer eyes of yellow-green. I carried one in my pocket for a long time, & wish I could have taken him away!

—*To Lillian D. Clark, 4–6 November 1924*

I should like to see the New-Englandish kittie at your place, & trust you will give him my best regards. Last night Morton brought a catnip mouse to the Boys' meeting at Belknap's, & we all watched to see what Felis would do with it. Would that habitual reserve & imperturbability be ruffled? Felis smelled the object, waved at it with a few graceful paw motions, rolled over once with the prize in his arms, & then calmly dropped it & walked out of the room! But humbler surroundings furnish sprightlier felines, & Kirk & I take a perennial delight in two small tiger-kittens at an Italian restaurant in Greenwich Village. They know us, & we each have one which we habitually hold. Kirk calls his Lucrezia Borgia, & I call mine Giambattista Tintoretto. Both are playful, & although growing rapidly do not yet amount to much more than a comfortable double-handful.

—*To Lillian D. Clark, 26 February 1925*

I don't rate the work of [Thomas] Hardy quite so high as most in this generation do, but I certainly endorse his feline tastes to the uttermost limit! Which reminds me that the other day I saw and stroked quite the most delightful large maltese cat imaginable in a doorway near here. How he did rub and purr! Grandpa's big grey boy! Give my regards to the black and the white cat when you see them again. I wonder which was really the *least* clean?

—*To Lillian D. Clark, 5 June 1925*

I [sought] Brooklyn to get some post cards & magazines, & incidentally petting two delectable tiger-kitties near the P.O. (I saw, by the way, the most captivating kitten boxing-match imaginable at Hunter's Island, where a family of one mother-kittie & two children were hunting field mice in a bank wall near a creek.) But the trip was to end in still more feline fashion—for just as I was passing Borough Hall I was greeted with the sight of the loveliest little coal-black nigger-baby that ever purred or said "meow"! Bless my old bones, but what a superbly tiny atom of unalloyed night that precious rascal was! Not a non-black hair on the little devil—& his face was exactly like my vanished Nigger-Man's! Well—there was only one thing a venerable priest of Pasht could do, so I picked the little imp up & held him in my lap a full hour as I sat on a bench & read about Bryan & his passing in the premature Monday morning papers.[*] He purred & snuggled & kneaded my knees with his little paws—in fact, it was all I could do not to kidnap him forthwith! I wonder whose he is? He was obviously contented, well fed, & cared for, though he had no collar. Grandpa's little pickaninny! Finally my young friend yawned & stretched & became uneasy, so I let him hop down to disappear in the kindred blackness of ingulphing night & join the witches' train in unhallow'd ceremonies.

—To Lillian D. Clark, 27 July 1925

My greetings to the felines you have met—may they flourish long & gloriously! I have seen many lately, but none to equal the little black boy of two weeks ago—whom I have sought assiduously tho' in vain in the neighbourhood of Borough-Hall.

—To Lillian D. Clark, 8 August 1925

---

[*] William Jennings Bryan, the lead prosecuting attorney during the Scopes trial in Dayton, Tenn., died a few days after the trial was concluded, on 26 July 1925.

I set forth on a nocturnal pilgrimage after mine own heart; beginning at Chelsea, the village overtaken by New-York in the 'forties, west of 7th Ave. between 18th & 24th Sts, & working south toward Greenwich amongst the curious houses, imagination-kindling streets, & innumerable kitty-cats whose graceful presence called back to memory the wholesome long-departed domestick life of the village. [. . .] Once I found a mother-cat with two of the tiniest imaginable black-&-white kittens—irresistibly lovely little rascals—& this time the temptation was too strong to resist . . . I put one of them in my (old blue) coat pocket, with his head out, & carried him around with me for nearly an hour; later returning to where I had found him, & depositing him on the steps from which his mamma & brother had vanished. He was the prettiest, most microscopic little rascal I've seen in years—big-eyed & alert, & prone to chew playfully at one's fingers. I saw many other small kittens during my jaunt—this must be the beginning of the fall crop, bless their little hearts! Grandpa's chilluns!

—To Lillian D. Clark, 13 August 1925

Starting among the dim streets under Brooklyn Bridge, we first encountered a tiny black-&-white kitten whose graces threatened to detain us indefinitely, & whose kidnapping we quite seriously discussed. *Such* a *little* kitty-cat!

—To Lillian D. Clark, 8 September 1925

I'd like to see that Maltese kittie you mention. Last night I stroked the most delightful Maltese imaginable in front of the James Monroe house—he was about half-grown, & purred & arched his back in a manner truly captivating. He seemed impressed with the antiquity & sanctity of his surroundings. Then on the homeward trip I saw a magnificent little black

& white boy by the subway entrance. Kirk is going to keep a kitty-cat in his new quarters, & has already picked out his companion—a tiny black fellow with a little white, now too young to leave his foster-mother, but to be delivered as soon as sufficiently grown. Needless to say, I am awaiting his advent with the keenest expectancy—he is an orphaned waif, who strayed into Kirk's favourite Downing St. restaurant just at the time when the old lady cat there was nursing her own tiger brood. Madam Tabitha, in a generous mood, added the forlorn mite to her household without the least hesitation; & there he now abides, awaiting the time when his Grandpa Georgius will be able to bear him away. Those Downing St. Italians cherish their felidae with an almost Egyptian tenderness which warms the heart! No kitten has ever been killed in that restaurant, but with each new brood a canvass of patrons is made with a view to providing homes. And not only have the homes been always forthcoming, but at one time the two kittens which the proprietor kept were *stolen*—one finding his way back, (well-nourished & evidently after a stay with kindly thieves) but the other remaining to this day a mourned & unsolved mystery.

—*To Lillian D. Clark, 18 September 1925*

I am about to start down to 14th St. to attend the reception in honour of the homecoming of our gang's official mascot—Edgar Evertsen Saltus Kirk, who this morning left his foster-mamma at the Downing St. restaurant & took up his abode with Uncle Georgius in Chelsea! He is black & white & exceedingly playful, so I am apprised over the telephone, & his master is going to round up as many of our circle as possible to welcome him & make him feel as much at home as a very small kitty-cat can feel in a vast pair of early-Victorian apartments.

I shall stop somewhere en route & get Edgar some catnip—which I trust he is old enough to appreciate. Verily, I am all impatience to behold this diminutive personage, & envy Kirk has ability in devising a working plan for harbouring a feline member of the family. I saw loads of fascinating kitties in Jamaica, Flushing, & Hempstead!

—*To Lillian D. Clark, 2 October 1925*

I cannot forbear beginning with my diary—which chronicles the pensive sequel to the affair of small Edgar Evertsen Saltus Kirk, to meet whom I was going down town when last I writ you. As outlined in that former communication, I indeed went down to 14th St., stopping on the way to purchase a catnip ball at a chemist's shop; & upon my arrival was greeted by Kirk, Loveman, & Leeds, together with an amiable & appealing stripling of the feline species, about ¾ grown, & white except for grey markings on ears, feet, & tail. Now this alert & sophisticated specimen was obviously not the black & white atom from Downing St., who had been too small to leave his foster-mother; & my host at once proceeded to explain the discrepancy. It seems that the Downing St. nursling is still too young to be taken, & that Kirk—out walking Thursday night with Loveman—saw this larger kitten in a Greenwich alley, becoming so captivated with him that he took him home & adopted him forthwith, on the principle that a cat in the home is worth two in the restaurant. The little rascal was delightfully playful & friendly, & revelled gracefully with the catnip ball I brought him before hopping up to sleep in Grandpa's lap. [. . .] And now the tragedy intervenes! About midway in our labours young Edgar Evertsen politely asked to be excused for a time, so that Kirk let him out the window. Moments pass'd, & he did not return—nor were any of the various searching-parties which we dispatch'd able to find him. Eheu! He had melted into that engulfing & uncommunicative night which had so lately yielded him up, & it is to be fear'd we shall never behold him more! The catnip ball rolls listlessly & mournfully about, & the piece of play-string pines for a little paw to chase it. I tell Kirk that Edgar probably had a good home to begin with, & has doubtless returned to it. Now he'll have to wait till that Downing-St. kitty-cat is old enough to leave his foster-mamma! [P.S.:] Loveman is here—I stayed in all the morning & now we're going on the trip. He brings news that *Edgar Evertsen has been back* to Kirk's & run away *again!!*

—*To Lillian D. Clark, 4 October 1925*

I enjoyed both the cuttings, & had previously noted the one about "Manna". His face looks like that of Oscar, a delightful neighbour of Kirk's, who occasionally drops in to call on the Kirk feline.

To Lillian D. Clark, 24–27 October 1925

Oscar—et tu! Gawd, but what is left to me in life! That's the darn trouble of growing old—all one's old pals start croaking one after the other, till the only place a bimbo can feel at home is in the cemetery. This very second I'm dropping a black-border'd card to the bereaved neighbour; asking for the SL & RK Elegies, & adding a less ambitious but equally sincere tribute worded thus:

> Damn'd be this harsh mechanick age
> That whirls us fast & faster,
> And swallows with Sabazian rage
> Nine lives in one disaster.

I take my quill with sadden'd thought,
Tho' falt'ringly I do it;
And, having curst the Juggernaut,
Inscribe: OSCARVS FVIT!
—*To James F. Morton, 28 June 1926*

[George Kirk] has a fine new cat—who sleeps at the foot of his bed—& a second cat who is a constant visitor but whom he does not technically own. This same feline is now on the table beside this sheet of paper, & has tracked some dust on it!
—*To Lillian D. Clark, [15 September 1926]*

The flat [of the writer Paul Allen] is at 88 Horatio St., in a semi-antique district, but not till we entered did I realise why Loveman had had me invited there. Then I saw the reason—& *what* a reason! Bless Grandpa's bones—*what* a 'ittle **kittie!!!** His name is "Boojum", & he is about two months old. His head is tigerish Maltese, his paws & tail are dark tiger, & the rest of him is white. His length is about 8 or ten inches . . . . yet within that brief compass what a cosmos of kinetic & fatigueless playfulness resides!! The precious little atom was not still a second, but rolled & chased & boxed & leaped & tumbled & cavorted all the evening without intermission. He climbed & chewed his way all over his Grandpa Theobald, & certainly kept the old gentleman well absorbed & entertained throughout the session. At odd moments my host's books, wife, old china, & furniture were pointed out to me. Tea, I believe, was served. But my one persistent impression is of small "Boojum". As adieux were exchanged, I was given the loan of a clothes-brush—at whose moving bristles Boojum leaped ecstatically even as I strove to remove his capillary vestiges. My wrists still bear the delicate tattooing of his delicate claws—& as I gaze reminiscently at the artless tracery I again give vent to the sententious reflection—*some* kitty-cat!

—To Lillian D. Clark, 23 May 1928

Glad the cat-&-dog sketch proved amusing.* I had a chance to prove my feline devotion last week at Little Belknap's, for the Child has lately secured a dog—a black Scotch Terrier—& all the family have combined to render it homage & neglect their regal & magnificent coon-cat Felis. I lost no opportunity to shew my unshaken preference for Felis, though at all times treating his canine rival with amiable civility. Felis is still Grandpa's boy—& I took pains to let everyone know it.

—To Elizabeth Toldridge, 4 May 1929

---

* "Cats and Dogs."

Old Man

So I *hadn't* spoken about "Old Man" & my dreams of him!
Well—he was a great fellow. He belonged to a market at the
foot of Thomas Street—the hill street mentioned in "Cthulhu"
as the abode of the young artist—& could usually (in later
life) be found asleep on the sill of a low window almost touch-
ing the ground. Occasionally he would stroll up the hill as
far as the Art Club, seating himself at the entrance to one of
those old-fashioned courtyard archways (formerly common
everywhere) for which Providence is so noted. At night, when
the electric lights made the street bright, the space within the
archway would remain pitch-black, so that it looked like the
mouth of an illimitable abyss, or the gateway of some nameless dimension. And there, as if stationed as a guardian of the
unfathomed mysteries beyond, would crouch the sphinxlike,
jet-black, yellow-eyed, & incredibly ancient form of Old Man.
I first knew him as a youngish cat in 1906, when my elder
aunt lived in Benefit St. nearby, & Thomas St. lay on my route
downtown from her place. I used to pet him & remark what
a fine boy he was. I was 16 then. The years went by, & I continued to see him off & on. He grew mature—then elderly—&
finally cryptically ancient. After about 10 years—when I was
grown up & had a grey hair or two myself—I began calling
him "Old Man". He knew me well, & would always purr &
rub around my ankles, & greet me with a kind of friendly
conversational "e-ew" which finally became hoarse with age.
I came to regard him as an indispensable acquaintance, &
would often go considerably out of my way to pass his habitual territory, on the chance that I might find him visible.
Good Old Man! In fancy I pictured him as an hierophant of

the mysteries behind the black archway, & wondered if he would ever invite me *through* it some midnight . . . . wondered, too, if I could ever come back to earth alive after accepting such an invitation. Well—more years slipped away. My Brooklyn period came & went; & in 1926, a middle-aged relique of 36, with a goodly sprinkling of white in my thatch, I took up my abode in Barnes Street—whence my habitual downtown route led straight down Thomas St. hill. And there by the ancient archway Old Man still lingered! He was not very active now, & spent most of his time sleeping—but he still knew his fellow-elder, & never failed to give his hoarse, friendly "e-ew" when he chanced to be awake. About 1927 he took on a sort of final second youth & began to be awake more. He had been sticking rather close to the market, but now I met him farther & farther up the hill, & very often at the old archway. Good Old Man! In 1928 he seemed a trifle feeble, but his purring friendliness was unabated. Not long before my 38th birthday I saw him—him whom I had known at 16. Then in August I began to miss him. Always when turning the corner on to the hill I used to look down ahead & see if I could discern a familiar lump of black by the archway or at the market. Now I failed to see the graceful old furry lump. I feared the worst—but scarcely dared to enquire at the market. At last—in September—I did enquire & found that my fears were all too well founded. After more than two decades Old Man had gone through the archway at last, & dissolved into that eternal night of which he was a true fragment—that eternal night which had sent him up to earth as a tiny black atom of sportive kittenhood so long ago! Assuredly, I felt desolate enough without my old friend—without any black lump to look for on the ancient hill. I had dreamed of him—& the mysteries of the archway—before; but I now began to do so with redoubled vividness. He would greet me in sleep on a spectral Thomas Street hill, & gaze with aged yellow eyes that spoke secrets older than Ægyptus or Atlantis. And he would mew an invitation for me to follow him through the archway—beyond which lay (as saith Dunsany) "the unreverberate darkness of the abyss."[*] In no dream up to now have I actually followed him through—but I have often wondered what will happen if ever I do . . . . . whether, in such an event, I shall ever again awake in this tri-dimensional world? When I mentioned these dreams to Dwyer he wanted to make a story about Old Man, but he has not yet done so. If he doesn't, I may myself some day. Good Old Man! But I am sure that no world he would lead me to would be a world of horror. He is too old & true a friend for that! When little Sam Perkins appeared on the scene last summer I decided that he must be a great-great-great-great-great-grandson of Old Man—perhaps a messenger despatched from the Abyss by my old friend. As soon as his great violet eyes began to turn yellow, I occasionally addressed him as Old Man, & fancied I could sense a spark of recognition! Perhaps he was my friend himself in a new body! But, alas, he did not remain long. He, too, returned to that eternal Night of which he & all his kind are inalienable fragments! Thanks, by the way, for immortalising little Sam in the name of your character. The Kappa Alpha Tau is investigating the hostile influence which seems to hover over the felidae this year; & as soon as we discover the daemon responsible for it, we shall call forth some very strange force through monstrous midnight incantations! All hands, by the way, send their sincerest regards to Crom, & express the hope that his indisposed paw may soon regain its pristine vigour.

—*To Duane W. Rimel, 22 December 1934*

_____

[*] The last line of Dunsany's "The Probable Adventure of the Three Literary Men"; quoted in HPL's "The Nameless City" (1921).

The Kappa Alpha Tau

I have two distinguished guests today—each a fair-sized handful. Little tiger kittens—eyes open, but still shaky in navigation & not playful yet. They belong in the boarding-house whose rear abuts on our back garden, & I fancy I shall borrow one or both of them quite frequently during the various stages of their sportive youth. Probably I mentioned that I am almost fanatically fond of cats.

—*To Robert Bloch, [22 July 1933]*

My two tiger cubs are now abridged to one—the weaker brother having come to another & better land where fields of catnip stretch away to oceans of salmon-peopled milk. But the remaining cub is surely some boy! Bless me, but how a week & a half has developed the little rascal! He's now strong & agile, & incredibly bright & playful. I borrow him often—so that he is coming to know these colonial corridors exceeding well. As for the canidae—I'm largely indifferent to them, though I have no active dislike. I despise their satellitism & slobbery habits as opposed to the bland independence & instinctive neatness & delicacy of the felidae. A comely black cat with large yellow eyes is to me about the apex of organic grace. Every motion & shade of posture is a poem in line & motion. But I like all the felidae.

—*To Robert Bloch, [late July 1933]*

One thing I like about this place is the refined & sedate club of felidae on the roof of a shed across the garden, in plain sight of my study windows. There are seldom fewer than one or two sleek old Toms at the "clubhouse", & occasionally as many as five or six or seven. Four of them belong to the antient gentlewoman residing two doors below here. In view of the prevalence of fraternity-houses in the neighbourhood, I am calling this pleasing sodality the Kappa Alpha Tau— which stands for Κομψῶν Αἰλουρῶν Τάξις.[*] The President (with whom I am become such good friends that he rolls over & kicks & purrs like a kitten upon my approach) is a huge, handsome black-&-white gentleman of antient lineage. The Vice-President is a gigantick tiger of prodigious dignity. The Secretary is a great Maltese with white spots. There is one very sprightly young fellow (also a Maltese), smaller than the rest of the boys, who is undergoing initiation.

—*To James F. Morton, 6 October 1933*

The Kappa Alpha Tau has several new members—a fine all-black fellow, a curious grey piebald chap, a rather pale tiger, a black &-white boy who I am sure must be Pres. Randall's son, a fat pale-yellow gentleman, & a trim tiger much like Vice-Pres. Osterberg. The black boy & the piebald display combative tendencies promising considerable entertainment. But there is bad news, too. Little Galpin—last July's handful of wobbly grey fur who grew to be such a friendly, sportive, & vociferously purr-ful visitor—has not been seen at his home for a week. I can't believe he has met with an accident, for he has never braved the streets outside our placid island of semi-rural and-whereness. Rather do I fancy he was stolen. I hope he has a good home.

—*To James F. Morton, 19 December 1933*

---

[*] Band of elegant or well-dressed cats.

Glad the felidae are prospering—Florida's genial clime seems to have a maturing effect on the youngsters! My friends on the shed roof below my window—the Kappa Alpha Tau fraternity—seem as sleek as ever . . . . the hardier ones appear frequently, though the venerable black & white president remains out of sight during the winter, being no doubt as reluctant as I am to leave a snug indoor hearth.

—To R. H. Barlow, [13 January 1934]

Here on the ancient hill, as I may have mentioned, I am in close touch with the secret & portentous Kappa Alpha Tau (Κομψῶν Αἰλουϱῶν Τάξις) fraternity which meets on the roof of a shed across the garden beneath my west window. The president, Peter Randall, is an elderly black & white gentleman of aristocratic & sacerdotal descent, who inherits the darkest arcana of Bubastis & Meroë. Like me, he is no lover of cold weather, but appears at the club only when climatic conditions are favourable. His aloofness from ordinary mortals both human & feline is proverbial, but he has at last permitted me to break through his reserve, so that he now even rolls over in an undignified & kittenish fashion when he sees Grandpa E'ch-Pi-El approaching. The Vice-President, Count Magnus Osterberg (belonging to a Scandinavian household in Waterman St.), is a huge & handsome tiger with a white face & gloves & boots, whose aristocratic reserve is quite equal to Pres Randall's. He & Peter are very close friends, but neither ever pays the slightest attention to any other feline. When one is out alone, he always looks about for the other; & when they have found each other they generally take up permanent stations about two feet apart—dozing, surveying the semi-rural scenery of their back-garden oasis, or exchanging courteous & affable glances. Casual approaches of other cats are unheeded, but when any outside Grimalkin becomes actually obtrusive & overbearing (no cat of K.A.T. calibre *would* become so!), Count Magnus displays the hardier side of his nature. (Pres. Randall has outlived his combative years, hence repels foes only with chilling glances.) Magnus never *picks* a fight, & often goes to considerable lengths of tact to avert a vulgar brawl—but when the other guy becomes insistent, so that a gentleman must either fight or bear the imputation of tarnished honour, then just watch the scion of the ancient Osterberg line! All the hardy blood of generations of Norrland jarls, & all the cryptic lore learnt from the Lapp & Finnish warlocks, then come to the fore—& the fur that flies during the ensuing moments is not often the tiger-&-white miniver of Count Magnus Osterberg! Just as I have never seen Count Magnus provoke or incite a combat, so have I never seen him retreat. A true gentleman & Nordic nobleman, by God! Both Pres. Randall & Vice Pres. Osterberg have their favourite spots for taking the air—the President favouring the clubhouse roof (which is in his yard) & Count Magnus his own back fence, slightly to the north. Each, however, is very courteous about transferring the seat of a colloquy to the other's chosen territory. As for the others—the secretary is a large Maltese, recently elected to replace a grey part Angora who has withdrawn from the fraternity. The Treasurer—Stephen Randall, who looks enough like Peter to be his son, though he has no white spot on the end of his tail—is also newly chosen, supplanting a small tiger who resigned. Other members are a titanic coal-black warrior with a stentorian voice, a pale yellow gentleman of fairly martial tastes, an exceedingly handsome double-pawed tortoise-shell, & a large, pale tiger—tolerated more or less on probation. When four or five are assembled on the clubhouse roof beneath my window, the effect is the most companionable kind of thing imaginable.

Count Magnus, moreover, sometimes honours this household with a visit. Of other local felidae—non-members of the Kappa Alpha Tau—one may mention the white & black huntress at the boarding-house across the back garden, who is my aunt's especial favourite. Last summer, after some of her own kittens were eliminated by the local Nazi committee which decided they didn't come up to the best Aryan standard, she adopted two exquisite little tigers with unopened eyes from some unknown source & proceeded to rear them with scientific solicitude. One was later given to appreciative owners, but the other (an utterly fascinating & incredibly companionable little rascal) became my most frequent visitor & constant playmate. Because of his sprightly, insolent precocity I called him *Alfred Galpin* after our iconoclastic young friend . . . . & how he did climb over my desk & chair & shoulders & all the surrounding points of vantage . . . . . threading his way over tables & among ornaments without ever breaking a thing! But alas! One sad day in mid-December he failed to appear in his wonted haunts, & he has never since been seen. All mourn his absence—& try to picture him as the recipient of some kindly rather than tragic fate. Perhaps he skipped & sidled toward one of our glorious hillside sunsets & passed into the fourth dimension, there to remain as an acolyte of the panther-god Hra in the City of Never, always as young as on the day he came. But it was a blow to the K.A.T. to lose so promising a future member. Count Magnus has vowed vengeance upon any Entity responsible for the disappearance!
—*To Clark Ashton Smith, [c. 11 February 1934]*

You must not fail to draw me at least sketchy likenesses of Dame Simaetha and Genl. Tabasco—for the more you say of them, the more interested I become! Dwyer has just sent me some fascinating snaps of his black imp—a veritable fragment of the eternal Night! I mentioned them to Count Magnus the other day as he crouched on his beloved back-fence, & his answering purrs & rubbings were eloquent of curiosity. But behold! There is news from Ulthar! Not many days ago Mrs. Spotty, the white & black lady at the boarding-house across the back garden (Alfred Galpin's foster-mother of last summer) was delivered of the liveliest & most fascinating set of triplets ever beheld on this side of the River Skai. Eyes just open. Two—both Maltese—are promised to discriminating ailurophiles elsewhere; but the third—white & black like mamma—will be retained & reared. It is needless to say that I shall do considerable friendly borrowing in the weeks to come, when little Belknap (as I shall call him) is less dependent on immediate maternal vicinage! I hope he will not follow little Alfred Galpin into the baffling abyss of invisibility! There's a fine black & white feline—Oswald—at Sultan Malik's new habitat!

—To Clark Ashton Smith, [c. 9 March 1934]

Did I transmit to you & Doodlebug the latest news from Ulthar? Three kittens at the boarding-house across the back garden—two maltese (which will be given to admirers elsewhere) & one white & black like his mother. The latter will be kept—& you can wager that I'll do a great deal of borrowing as the weeks go by! Meanwhile the preliminary stirrings of Spring have begun to bring the sleek old Toms of the Kappa Alpha Tau out of hibernation.

—To R. H. Barlow, [19 March 1934]

Speaking of Ulthar & its colonies—I am infinitely your debtor for that haunting & subtly disquieting likeness of the daemon-link'd Simaetha! Verily, I can glimpse the latent nightmare in those slitlike, widely-spaced eyes! It is clear that those eyes have look'd upon things whose very mention would blast a common mortal. When you can corner the belligerent & elusive General I'd appreciate a sketch of him as well—for I feel that there must be a vast amount of hearty likeability in the bluff old veteran. By the way—a friend of mine named John Quincy Adams, who lives at Adams' Market farther north on the ancient hill & spends most of his time at the Art Club next door, has just suffered a severe mauling & tearing . . . . . the result of an argument with a moving motor. He's recovering, though—despite a limp. Mr. Adams is generally to be found curled up on an ancient chest in the main gallery of the Art Club; & he knows Grandpa E'ch-Pi-El so well that he comes over and jumps in the Old Gentleman's lap when the latter sits down. He is a huge tiger with a touch of Persian or Angora, & retains the playful & affectionate disposition of a kitten despite his undeniable middle age. With suitable encouragement, he even rolls over on his back & kicks! Spring weather is swelling the attendance at the K.A.T. meetings, & Pres. Randall is now to be found regularly on his favourite shed roof . . . . . . usually with Count Magnus just two feet away. The grey twins across the garden, alas, left for their new home last Monday . . . . I hope they'll like it. When I get home from my wanderings their little white & black brother here will be a very big boy!

—*To Clark Ashton Smith, [c. 13 April 1934]*

At the boarding-house across the back garden I found something else of infinite interest and grace—something small and coal-black and furry, that is still a bit wobbly on its little legs, although already beginning to be playful. Just a double-handful with great eyes undecided whether to turn green or yellow . . . . Mrs. Spotty Perkins's latest child, born last month and known as Samuel. Yesterday young Mr. Perkins spent a couple of hours at #66, crawling all over Grandpa, chewing the old gentleman's fingers and coat-lapels, and finally dropping off to sleep whilst Grandpa read the *Evening Bulletin*. He hasn't begun to purr yet, but probably will shortly. Grandpa's little nigger-man! He looks like a bear cub of paperweight size . . . . I must get a photograph of the microscopick rascal! He's certainly slated to spend a lot of time over at 66! When he grows up he'll doubtless join the Kappa Alpha Tau on the shed roof beyond the side garden. Incidentally—Mrs. Spotty's February kitten—Betsey Perkins, an almost precise black and white duplicate of herself—is getting to be quite as big as mamma, though she still seeks nourishment at the maternal bosom along with little brother Sam.

—*To Maurice W. Moe, 17 July 1934*

The black kitten across the back garden continues to be a frequent visitor—had him over all yesterday evening. He is certainly an imp from Azathoth's nethermost gulf of tenebrous chaos!

—*To Robert Bloch, [late July 1934]*

The feline news is welcome. I'm not surprised at Low's choice of a cradle for her young, since she seemed to show quite a partiality for that comfortable sagging roof-canvas last month. Rockabye, baby, on the shed's top! But you ought to see the little black devil whom I now have as my guest! He's been racing & rolling among my papers till my desk-top looks something like yours, & now he's curled up in my lap resting. He has grown spectacularly since my return home, & is now a tiny dynamo of pep—racing about the garden in the shadows, boxing with his mother, & leaping frantically at paper on the end of strings. The once-ratty little tail is getting handsomely bushy, & the youthful throat is just getting warmed up to the act of purring. I surely hope that nothing will happen to the little rascal—his big black & white sister Betsey, born last February, disappeared 3 days ago to the universal mourning of the boarding-house's inhabitants.

—*To R. H. Barlow, [3?–6 August 1934]*

Little Sam Perkins continues to be an important figure in the neighbourhood of 66 College. He was ill a week ago—languid & drooping—but is now quite his dynamic little self again. He purrs off & on, but not very steadily. His eyes are turning out to be yellow, & his face is one of the prettiest I have ever seen. Altogether, he is an unimaginably graceful little piece of the night! I've tried to snap him twice, but shan't know how well or ill I've succeeded till the film is developed. You'll be sorry to hear that his big sister Betsey has suddenly disappeared—a very singular thing, since she never went out of the garden & on the streets where she might be run over. The people at the boarding house are quite disconsolate. As for the name—an old lady at the boarding house* started the *Perkins* business last February when Betsey & her 2 brothers were born. For some reason or other—perhaps because "Perkins" has a kind of quaint, old-fashioned sound—she named the black & white kitten "Betsey Perkins", though leaving the others (slated for presentation to a family across the city) undesignated. I, however, called the little fellows "Newman Perkins" & "Ebenezer Perkins" after ancestors of my own—for I have a Perkins line. When the black kitten appeared, I went back along my Perkins ancestry & called him Samuel, after a forbear who fought

---

* I.e., Marian F. Bonner residing at The Arsdale at 55 Waterman Street, just behind HPL's residence.

in King Philip's War in 1676. If there are any more kittens later on, I shall probably keep going back along my Perkins line (which is traceable to 1380 in Shropshire & Warwickshire) for names—*John* being the next in order. But I seldom call a cat by any *one* name. When I speak to little Sam I call him all sorts of things—"Little Black Devil", "Old Nigger Man", "Spawn of the Shadows", "Little Piece of the Night", "Old Black Panther", "Little Onyx Sphinx", "Child of Bast", & so on, & so on . . . . . not excluding the succinct & universal "kittie"!

—*To Duane W. Rimel, 10 August 1934*

Snaps of the kittens will be highly welcome—I'd like to see the little imps now that they've descended to earth & acquired the lively graces of their kind. I've taken two snaps of little Sam Perkins, but don't know whether they're any good. 4 more views to be taken on the film. The tiny black devil simply can't be kept still! He was ill the other day, but is now quite his dynamic self again. I never saw such a concentrated bundle of energy before—the imp is even more restless than you are! He purrs a great deal now—& will be doing it like a house afire in another week. I borrow him constantly, & he & his mother play for hours around the chair in the garden where my aunt sits on sunny afternoons.

—*To R. H. Barlow, [14 August 1934]*

As for little Sam Perkins—you ought to see him *now!* Bless Grandpa's bones, what a little black dynamo of ceaseless sportive energy! Of all little imps of Beëlzebub . . . . & how he can purr! I have him over at 66 nearly all the time, but his folks don't seem to mind!

—*To Elizabeth Toldridge, 31 August 1934*

I regret vastly to hear that one of the new felidae has had disastrous differences with Doodlebug, & hope fervently that he may emerge triumphant from his injuries. Little Sam Perkins—across the garden from 66—is a great hand at offering fight to the stately gentlemen of the Kappa Alpha Tau, but so far none of the latter has taken him up. They're good sportsmen enough to pick a fellow of their size! Much the same is true of the young tiger angora—Peter Ivanovitch—at Cole's house where I visited. This lively little devil constantly sails into staid old grey & white Napoleon & tiger Duke of Wellington—but he seems to put these greybeards to rout rather than inspire savage reprisals!

—*To R. H. Barlow, 1 September 1934*

But the saddest news is yet to come. Alas—how can I impart it unmov'd? Little Sam Perkins, the tiny ball of black fur whom you saw in August, is no more! He was ill then—but fully recover'd & was quite his usual dynamick little self. As late as Sept. 7 he spent the day with Grandpa—tearing about the place, shuffling the papers on the old gentleman's desk, & finally stretching out like a little ebony stick in the semicircular chair, sound asleep. On the morning of the 10th, however, he was found peacefully lifeless in the garden—& from no apparent cause. Now he sleeps beneath the shrubbery amidst which he play'd in life. Blessed little piece of the Night! He liv'd but from June to September, & will never know what the winter's hellish cold is like. The Kappa Alpha Tau is in deep mourning, & President Randall often news in elegiack numbers—

> The ancient garden seems tonight
> A deeper gloom to bear,
> As if some silent shadow's blight
> Were hov'ring in the air.

> With hidden griefs the grasses sway,
>   Unable quite to word them—
> Remembering from yesterday
>   The little paws that stirr'd them.

During his later days Master Perkins was fully inducted into the K.A.T.—appearing frequently on the clubhouse roof. Eheu—the old place is not the same without him!
                              —*To James F. Morton, 24 September 1934*

News from #66 is neither interesting nor cheerful. In the first place, I'm just pulling out of a hellish siege of indigestion which had me in bed—or dragging betwixt there & the kitchen & bathroom—a week, & good for nothing a week more. And in the second place the Kappa Alpha Tau & I are mourning the loss of our brightest & sprightliest scion—none other than little Sam Perkins himself! He was found lifeless in the ancient garden on September 10th, & now sleeps beneath the grasses amidst which he loved to play in life. And as late as Sept. 7 he was over here climbing around Grandpa's shoulders & chewing the papers on the desk! He had had a spell of illness early in August, & this must have been some obscure & aggravated recurrence. Blessed little Piece of the Night—Tsathoggua's youngest & tiniest son! In his momentary flash of existence—June to September—he never learned the horrors of winter or the seething vortex of modernity beyond the confines of his own garden oasis. And who shall say the gods found him less important than the longest-lived & worldliest philosopher? During his last weeks he became fully initiated into the Kappa Alpha Tau, so that his little black presence was often seen on the clubhouse roof beside the ampler bulk of black-&-white Pres. Randall & tiger Vice-Pres. Osterberg. But all things pass—& today Mrs. Spotty Perkins hunts mice &

chases grasshoppers childless & alone! I am sure that mother Simaetha & Genl. Tabasco will share the grief of their eastern kin. Pray give them my regards—& let us hope that their effectiveness in guarding Indian Hill against the Things from Outside may never wane!

— To Clark Ashton Smith, [c. 30 September 1934]

I dream of cats very often—did I ever mention my curious dreams about the ancient black sage who used to greet me daily at the entrance of one of the quaint colonial archways on the hill? He died in 1928 at an age substantially over 20 yrs. Dwyer once had an idea of weaving a story around him. I've dreamed several times about little Sam Perkins, & was pleased to see his name in your new story!* The Kappa Alpha Tau are still eloquent in expressing their appreciation of your verses. As for the ill-fortune attending the feline population this autumn—it is really getting to be quite uncanny! The latest victim is the faithful tiger companion of my revision-client Mrs. Heald—who ate some Paris green in the cellar, was seized with a sort of frenzy, & dashed out of the house, never to be seen again. No further reports concerning Doodlebug or Gen. Tabasco—alas! But the K.A.T.'s original elders are still flourishing. Owing to the lateness of the season Pres. Randall (whose climatic tastes are like mine) is visible only on exceptional days, but Vice-Pres. Osterberg is a fixture at all times. Of late I've seen a stranger about—grey, plump, & rather youngish—but don't know whether he'll be voted in or not. Another new friend of mine—who I think is connected with the University Club at Benefit & Waterman streets—is quite young, & all black except for a small white star on his chest. He follows me quite a way up the hill when I pass his presumable

---

* "The Forbidden Room" (*Fanciful Tales*, Fall 1936).

abode, & is the most effusive & amicable of ankle-rubbers. But I haven't lately seen my huge tiger friend John Quincy Adams at the grocery next the Art Club. He had an accident a year ago, but was supposed to be recovering very nicely from it. Glad to hear that Crom continues to prosper! May he have as long & peaceful a life as Messrs. Randall & Osterberg appear to be having!

— *To Duane W. Rimel, 19 November 1934*

Speaking of my favourite species — the local Kappa Alpha Tau has begun to reassemble on the clubhouse roof . . . . . & best of all, a glorious brother & successor to my late friend Samuel Perkins (June–Sept. 1934) was born on St. Valentine's day at the boarding-house across the back garden. Little Johnny Perkins! What a boy! Coal-black except for a little white stud in the front of his fascist shirt-bosom! And what a spunky little divvle! He's only a single-handful still, but he hisses manfully at any intrusive finger poked his way, & boxes like a veteran not only with his proud mamma but with sundry visitors like his grandpa H P. I shall certainly be an extensive borrower of the young gentleman during the weeks & months to come! He is beginning to play, but doesn't purr yet — & the tip of his sable tail still retains something of the ratty pointedness of infancy. He's much firmer on his feet than most kittens of his age, & I fancy he'll grow into a first-rate fighting Tom. I hope he'll take care of his health & avoid the untimely demise encountered by little brother Sam!

— *To R. H. Barlow, [16 March 1935]*

Trust you'll decide to take both Xerxes & Artabanus to the trans-lacustrine hermitage. Mr. John Perkins is getting to be a great boy — & was here on a visit all day yesterday. He is developing a resonant purr, & is more wildly playful every day. He'll be a valiant warrior some time—though he is likewise engagingly friendly, now & then jumping up on Grandpa & promenading all over the old gentleman. It is fascinating to watch him in the garden among the greenery, playing by himself or with his mother.

—To R. H. Barlow, [11? May 1935]

Mr. John Perkins has become almost as great a frequenter of 66 as of his own home across the garden. He loves to chew papers on my desk, curl up in a neighbouring chair, or perch himself like a little basalt sphinx on top of Webster's Unabridged. He plays furiously, & is so pugnacious that he'll probably win the overlordship of the local K.A.T. by the time he's middle-aged. By the time I'm back from De Land he'll be a full-fledged warrior! The enclosed pictures of him & of Little Sam represent opposite ends of a roll of film started last August & finished in April. To think that these little brothers (*full* brothers, I am certain, for there can be little question about the lithe coal-black troubadour who appears to be their common sire) never existed at the same time!

—To Duane W. Rimel, 30 June 1935

Johnny Perkins welcomed me upon my return—but it took me some time to recognise the overgrown young rascal! Bless me, what a boy! He's going to be a huge warrior indeed before he's through. He is just as handsome as ever on an enlarged scale, & his coat is the sleekest, purest black I have seen in many an age. His late brother Sam had tiger-stripes shewing through, but John is absolute polished ebony except for his little snow-white necktie. He has been over at 66 a good part of the time since my arrival—purring & drowsing & playing.

We've got some catnip for him, which he has learned to relish exceedingly. News of his diminutive half-sister is tragic. She departed for her new home in mid-August—but fell a victim to motor traffic only about a week after the removal. The speeding car surely is the Kappa Alpha Tau's greatest enemy!
—*To Duane W. Rimel, 28 September 1935*

My black friend John Perkins of the Kappa Alpha Tau's younger generation is drowsing in a neighboring chair, & sends his regards to the venerable Simaetha. He is a very big boy now, but in many ways recalls the infinitesimal inky atom of last spring. Grandpa gives him catnip every time he comes to call, & he has developed a keen sense of gratitude—& anticipation. He has now has 3 little brothers at the boarding-house, for all of whom good homes have been found. One coal-black, two black & white. I shall enjoy watching the furry mites until their age permits them to leave the maternal breast & migrate to their new abodes.
-*To Clark Ashton Smith, [10 November 1935]*

Kappa Alpha Tau sends regards to Simaetha. One of Johnny's little brothers lingers on here—I wish they'd keep him permanently! His upper half is black, & his lower white—a quaint effect. Johnny cuffs him around, but he seems to like it! Possibly the Peacock Sultan has told you of valiant Nimrod's disappearance & return after 5 weeks. Old Nim certainly deserves to be the national K.A.T. president!
—*To Clark Ashton Smith, [2 December 1935]*

As I write, an especial friend of mine in the depths of a neighbouring easy-chair stirs in his slumbers & emits a few drowsy purrs. He is a huge black person, yet has never seen any year but 1935—having been born on the 14ᵗʰ of last February. Possibly I described him to you last spring as a tiny handful of black fur—but bless me, how the rascal has grown! Little Johnny Perkins! He belongs at the boarding-house across the back garden, but spends a good deal of his time over here. He knows who gives him catnip to chew & roll in—so he's a great friend of Grandpa's! He remembered me perfectly after my 3-month absence.

—*To J. Vernon Shea, 5 December 1935*

Glad to hear that Simaetha still flourishes. I feel very much bereft though the moving-away of the venerable black & white president & tiger vice-president of the local Kappa Alpha Tau chapter—these gentlemen having accompanied their human family to another neighbourhood. I look wistfully at the deserted clubhouse roof! But Mr. John Perkins still flourishes & often visits his old Grandpa Ech-Pi-El—& his smaller brother, Gilbert John Murray Kynymond Elliot, Earl of Minto,* likewise adorns the local scene. Lord Minto is black & white, & promises to become a very distinguished K.A.T. member.

—*To Clark Ashton Smith, [24 January 1936]*

The local Kappa Alpha Tau has sustained a devastating blow—though not from the stern hand of death. Old Pres. Randall & his tiger brother have *moved away* with their human family, leaving the clubhouse roof lone & desolate. I mourn, with many a wistful glance out the window! There will have to be a new election of officers in the spring, & I shall nominate Mr. John Perkins for President. Mr. Perkins—now a huge gentleman indeed—will be a year old day after tomorrow. For Vice-President I shall nominate his sprightly little broth-

---

* John Murray Kynynmond, 4th Earl of Minto (1845–1914), Governor-General of Canada (1898–1904) and Viceroy of India (1905–10).

er—Gilbert John Murray Kynymond Elliot, 4th Earl of Minto. Lord Minto is getting to be a great boy!

—*To Duane W. Rimel, 12 February 1936*

Mr. Perkins is indeed flourishing—& so is his younger brother Gilbert John Murray Kynymond Elliot, 4th Earl of Minto. Lord Minto was born in September, & is still very playful. He was named by one of his friends in the boarding house who spends the summer in New Brunswick & was a great admirer of the 4th Earl during his governor-generalship of Canada. The feline Gilbert is black & white, & presents a very graceful aspect. He was intended to be given away, but at the last moment the boarding-house decided to keep him. I am surely glad of his continued presence in these parts, for the local feline element has just been depleted by the removal from the neighbourhood of two of my favourite furry patriarchs—whose human family migrated elsewhere.

—*To Elizabeth Toldridge, 15 March 1936*

Just saw Johnny Perkins & gallant John Murray Kynymond Elliot around the fence near the clubhouse. Hope they intend to join the Kappa Alpha Tau. ¶ Have just secured Gilbert John as a guest—he is busy devouring catnip from the *new* box—but I can't for the life of me capture the Big Black Bum! The rascal is too agile for an old man! ¶ The 4th Earl is extremely companionable, & has just rolled over in his catnip as Big Brother used to do. And *what* a big boy he is getting to be! You must have him for a guest when you get back. ¶ Gilbert just asked to go, so Grandpa let him out. He has a full-throated mew wholly unlike Big Brother's little "ew". Hope he'll call again! ¶ The two brothers are now cavorting around the back garden. If I weren't going out for po'k & beans I'd try to catch that Big Black Bum again! ¶ Got my bek bin—*with* pork. Upon my return I found that good old Spotty had joined her sons, & was calling piteously to Gilbert John to cease his explorations of the clubhouse's interior. Gilbert is evidently a hard boy to manage!

—To Annie E. P. Gamwell, 21 March 1936

Have had a change of company since beginning this epistle. Mr. Perkins expressed a wish to return home (or at least to rove in the sunlit garden), but I have since caught his little brother—Gilbert John Murray Kynymond Elliot, fourth Earl of Minto—who is black on top & white on the bottom. Lord Minto was born last October, & will be a pretty big boy when you see him in September. He is now purring in the Morris-Chair in the corner—which is his favourite, just as the green-cushion'd semicircular chair is Mr. Perkins's favourite.

—To James F. Morton, 9 May 1936

Hope Sotho will soon be used to it—though he will doubtless retain a reminiscent fondness for his earlier abode. Glad he holds his own as local K.A.T. president. The Providence Chapter is flourishing under the leadership of Mr. Perkins (a year old last February) & his younger black & white brother the Earl of Minto. The spirited playing of the brothers in the garden is a delectable sight—& I fancy little Minto's influence helps to keep John in a kitten-like mood. Both the boys often come over to visit Grandpa—& I enjoy it especially when the two of them call at once & transfer their friendly gambols & graceful slumbering to my study.

—To Duane W. Rimel, 18 May 1936

The long, cold spring has worn my energies down to the vanishing-point, & I feel as if I were on the brink of some nervous explosion! An aggravating influence is the loss of my two best friends. Three weeks ago both Mr. John Perkins (black, born Feby. 14, 1935. You saw him last year) & the Earl of Minto (black & white—born last October) succumbed to some malady which is afflicting the local felidae—a thing which may be an obscure epidemic propagated by what you biologists call "filterable viruses", yet which may be the malign activities of some contemptible poisoner. The sad end of the brothers seemed connected with some digestive disorder. If this *is* the work of some wretched neo-Borgia, I hope to hell somebody feeds him poison a thousandfold more painful than that with which he has subtly supplied his innocent furry victims! For a time it looked as if there would never be any more kittens at the house across the garden—since a couple of months ago the white-&-black matriarch of the clan was given away to the psychological laboratory of Brown University . . . . where it was assumed she would round out her days in ease & luxury & academic dignity (together with other felidae, canidae, &c.) in tests of instinct, intelligence, perception, &c. for the benefit of successive generations of students. However, after the great dual bereavement the master of the establishment got her back—& now she roves the ancient garden once again, drawing the admiring glances of sundry black & tiger & maltese swains of the neighborhood. I hope she will prove true to the lean, black Mr. Perkins Senior, since I'd like to see another little black handful of fur like the late Johnny around here some time in the autumn!

—*To Kenneth Sterling, 20 June 1936*

[Anthem of the Kappa Alpha Tau]

Here we are,
The Kappa Alpha Tau boys;
We'll give a great meow, boys,
For Bast, and Sekhmet too.
Near and far,
We gather here as fellows,
And none may e'er excel
The Kappa Alpha Tau!

Here we shine,
The Kappa Alpha Tau boys;
Brave soldiers all allow, boys,
With many a victory.
Foes canine
In vain may seek to flout us,
For naught can ever rout
The Kappa Alpha Tau!

—From a letter to E. Hoffmann Price,
7 August 1934

Musings of an Ailurophile

[The following are extracts from HPL's letters to Marian F. Bonner, HPL's neighbour, who lived in a boarding house, The Arsdale, at 55 Waterman Street, across the back yard from HPL's home at 66 College Street.—Ed.]

1 April 1936:

[. . .] regarding the term by which your kindly and delightful fellow-inhabitant of The Arsdale was described. The word was *ailurophile,* and signifies one who, like myself, possesses an extreme fondness for the feline species. It is, of course, derived from the Greek αιλουρος, a cat—this term meaning literally "wag-tail", from αιλος, quick-moving or changeable (cf. Αιολος—Lat. Aeolus—the God of the Winds), and ουρα, tail. (If it be objected that the felidae are not habitual tail-waggers, except in anger or disapproval, I respectfully refer you to Mr. John Perkins of The Arsdale, whose eloquent caudal appendage is in a constant state of gentle vivacity even when he is most contentedly rounding out a catnip gorge.) I cannot guarantee the presence of this word in Webster (I have no edition later than 1890, and this gives only the word *ailuroidea,* a zoölogical term signifying the general catlike group of carnivora), but it has in the last twelve years been greatly popularised by the amiable and innocuous Professor William Lyon Phelps in his "As I Like It" column of *Scribners* (vide periodical room, P.P.L.)[*]; this eminent Victorian being

---

[*] I.e., the Providence Public Library.

himself enthusiastically ailurophilic.* The coinage of the word follows the most regular laws of philology— αιλουϱος, cat, and φιλεο, I love. Whether any singular word αιλουϱοφιλος exists in Greek to signify "cat-lover" I am frankly ignorant. It is not, however, in the tattered unabridged Liddell and Scott** which I inherited from my uncle. But if it did not exist in the classic Attic speech, this surely signifies a grave oversight on the part of the ancients. Professor Phelps' employment of this word took my attention most keenly when I first noticed it in 1924, since I had myself, through independent coinage, been habitually using it for years. Incidentally, I may remark that the word αιλουϱος figures in the name of the *Kappa Alpha Tau* fraternity of sleek old Toms which meets on the shed roof in the ex-Randall yard across the garden from my west windows. Whilst the superficial tend to give a commonplace phonetic interpretation to the initials K.A.T., I always correct this error by informing them that the name really signifies Κομψων Ἀιλουϱων Τάξις—i.e., a band or company of elegant or well-drest felidae. The dense ignorance of the majority is surprising and discouraging!

17 April 1936:

Aye, it is indeed lonely without ex-President Peter Randall—& his tiger brother Stephen, who so closely resembled the late Count Magnus Osterberg. Even now I occasionally forget their departure, & look expectantly at the clubhouse roof to see if any of my old friends are there. Old Peter was always like me—never visible in cold weather! He, by the way, was the first living being I ever saw in these ancient gardens, <u>when exploring</u> them three years ago with a view to future

---

* See note on p. 62.

** Henry George Liddell (1811–1898) and Robert Scott (1811–1887), *A Greek-English Lexicon* (1843). Still the standard Greek-English lexicon.

tenancy. In those days he fled at my approach—but in time he came to know & tolerate the other old gent, & would purr & roll over when Grandpa drew nigh . . . still imbued with some sportive recollection of his long-vanished kittenhood. And *what* a kitten he must have been, with that white spot at the tip of his tail!

26 April 1936:

Turning to recent topics in logical order—pray extend my sincerest gratitude to Pres. Perkins for his appointment of me as Official Limner of the local K.A.T. chapter. I shall proceed with the initial task—the portraits of all the members— just as soon as I can induce the latter (including the restless executive himself) to grant me suitable sittings. The list of suggested poses has been very carefully filed, & is most profoundly appreciated. Some are capable of very diverse treatment—thus *cat-a-comb* may signify either something like the Canal St. Station of the B.M.T. subway in New-York, or some process like that which my Florida friend Barlow applies to his Persian companions Cyrus & Darius when their acquisitive interest in entomology seems excessive.

22 May 1936:

The K.A.T. president & vice-president seem to bear up well despite the absence of the Chief Ailourophile—indeed, they are sometimes so lively in their garden gambols that it's rather hard for an old man to catch them! They both paid me a visit not long since—indeed, I wish they might decide to adopt #66 as one of their major clubhouses!

Extracts from Letters

I had a visitor the other night, who gave me an idea for a good story. He was a furry, four-footed young visitor, with a black coat, white gloves & boots, & white around the tip of his nose & the tip of his tail. He sat in a chair near me, purring most inspiringly, when I permitted my fancy to consider his ancient race & heritage. I am intensely fond of his species, as I have doubtless told you more than once; & as I looked upon him my thoughts ran thus:

. . . . . The cat is the soul of antique Ægyptus, & bearer of tales from forgotten empires in Meroë & Ophir. He is the kin of the jungle's lords, & heir to the secrets of hoary & sinister Africa. The Sphinx is his cousin, & he speaks her language; but he is more ancient than the Sphinx, & remembers that which she hath forgotten. . . . .

As I mused, a plot took form in my mind. A simple, yet a ghastly plot. And that plot will some day reach the amateur publick in the form of a tale to be entitled "The Cats of Ulthar".

—*To Rheinhart Kleiner, 21 May 1920*

In cataloguing the inhabitants of 20 Webster Street* one should not forget the maltese feline gentleman who goes by the appellation of "Tat"—a word coined in the dim past by the eldest of the now grown, wedded, and departed Sawyer boys. That has a reputation for wildness and fear of strangers, but before I left he permitted me to pick him up, and sat

---

* In Allston, Mass., joint residence of the amateur journalists Edith Miniter and Charles A. A. Parker.

contented in my lap, purring sleepily. He is exactly the colour of my new Outlet suit, so I would not have minded his shedding—but as it happened, he did not shed. I am told that I am the first stranger to succeed in holding him—but cats are my especial province, anyway!

—*To Sarah Susan Lovecraft, 17 March 1921*

After this non-essential digression the evening assumed more of the aspect of an ordinary amateur gathering, the company being augmented by the arrival of W. V. J., Miss Crist, Mrs. Wurtz, & a neighbour of Mrs. McMullen's** whose name has slipped my memory but who ought to be remembered for the menagerie which she brought with her—two large collie dogs, & the most exquisite *kitten* I have beheld in aeons. Mrs. McMullen averred that the latter small gentleman was brought especially in my honour, my liking for the feline species being well known in amateurdom. He was a greyish person of infinitely handsome features & longish hair, & a bushy tail suggesting a drop or two of Angora blood. Around his neck was a quaint collar with tiny bells; & as he gracefully moved, his antics pleased both eye & ear. He must have been about two or three months old—a good double handful in size—& he remained in his Grandpa Theobald's lap during most of the evening, chewing my vest buttons or fingers according to his youthful taste. Musical features were introduced, & the kitten pricked up his ears in vast & attentive interest, whilst the dogs dozed in a positively bourgeois fashion.

—*To Annie E. P. Gamwell, 19 August 1921*

Tryout's cat—Thomas II—is no more. He was run over by a

** The amateur poets Winifred Virginia Jackson and S. Lilian McMullen, who wrote under the pseudonym "Lilian Middleton." Miss Crist and Mrs. Wurtz are unidentified.

motor. Requiescat in pace!
—*To Lillian D. Clark, 13 August 1925*

Sorry you don't like the lap dogs—I think I like them the best of all dogs, since they are the most like cats. But I always prefer the real article, hence am much more interested in your bobtailed Maine neighbour with the sable coat & yellow eyes. Is his *decauditation* a natural feature, or has accident play'd its tragick role with him? If the former, I should say he had a strain of Manx blood—Maine cats are very mixed, a strong strain of Persian being responsible for the celebrated "coon cat" of which Belknap's "Felis" is the specimen *par excellence.*
—*To Lillian D. Clark, 7 November 1925*

I am interested to hear that the Maine kitty-cat is an acknowledged Manx. Bless me, but I'd like to see him! And too, I'd like to see the visiting black kittie of more longicaudate proportions. The dogs must be fairly interesting—& I agree that the black Pomeranian is to be preferred to the (theoretically) white poodle. But to me, a good—or even a fairly good—cat is to be preferr'd to both!
—*To Lillian D. Clark, 14–19 November 1925*

I'm glad you like "The Cats of Ulthar", & hope the public may do the same. [. . .] No doubt a reading of "Ulthar" promotes one's sense of weirdness as one listens to a feline conflict—possibly suggesting that the object attacked is not one of the cat tribe, but rather some powerful enemy of the species! I've always had another cat story in mind, which I may write some day—about a mother-kittie whose offspring are ruthlessly drowned, & who in turn effects the drowning of an infant child of the one who drowned her children. So

you still have the poor little Manx kittie! I rejoice in his little brother, still intact, which you so kindly sent, & in the others of the same family which cluster around. Really, you ought to see the cat section of my museum! Enclosed is a kittie-cutting which Belknap gave me recently. I wish I could see the two whose manoeuvres you watch from your window!
—*To Lillian D. Clark, 11 January 1926*

At Uncle James's place [i.e., the house of HPL's great-uncle James Phillips in Foster, R.I.] I continued some observations on the feline part of the population which I had begun in Moosup Valley, & decided that the prevalence of tailless Manx Cats was mark'd enough to constitute a distinct local feature. Evidently the breed secured a strong foothold at an early date, diffusing its blood throughout the continuously settled territory adjacent, but stopping when the distances became extreme. These uncaudal creatures are lively & graceful, & one soon forgets the handicap impos'd upon them by Nature—an handicap, indeed, which we poor featherless bipeds are not asham'd to share!
—*To James F. Morton, [late October 1926]*

As to the remarks of Mr. O'Higgins *de catis canibusque,*[*] I may rejoin that they are no more or less beside the point than most remarks based upon such false arts as phrenology, psycho-analysis, palmistry, & the like. As a matter of fact, most attempts to classify cat & dog lovers exactly according to social & philosophick standing must necessarily fail because of the essential complexity of the human mind. All we may say is, that the more purely an aesthete a man is, the more likely he is to prefer cats; since the superior grace, beauty, manners

---

* Harve O'Higgins appears to be an amateur journalist, possibly a member of the Blue Pencil Club. The term *catis* is, of course, a false Latin ablative plural for *cat* (more properly *felibus*).

& neatness of the cat cannot but conquer the fancy of any impartial observer emancipated from mundane & ethical illusions. In reality the purely aesthetick factors far outweigh the philosophick; so that although a gentleman *respects* a cat for its independence, aloofness, sufficiency, & coolness, he really *likes* the cat principally because of its peerless beauty & the superior gentleness & cleanness of its habits as compared with those of the noisy, smelly, pawing, slobbering, messy dog. It has a charm & a poise & a classic restraint which dogs totally lack, & its appeal to the imagination is tremendous—all this wholly apart from any question of affection, devotion, dependence, aloofness, superiority or inferiority. Really, no cat-lover of sound sense need appeal at all to the treacherous catch words of psychology. All that is required is to establish a standard of pure beauty without subsidiary encumbrances, & the cats have it in a walk! We love kitties, gawd bless their little whiskers, & we don't give a damn whether they or we are superior or inferior! They're confounded pretty, & that's all we know & all we need to know! But of course one must rationalise & philosophise & draw ponderous inferences for publick perusal in a world of heavy mental superfluities, so articles like mine & Mr. Van Doren's will continue to be written.

—*To James F. Morton, [December] 1926*

As for kitty-cats—I agree that they are essentially a masculine animal: a delight of unsentimental & disillusioned aesthetes who appreciate abstract beauty of line & motion without reference to the petty quality of fawning affection for mankind. I saw the article you clipped in my Bulletin, & shewed it to regal old Felis—who spat in critical acknowledgment! I'd like to see the Maltese you mention.

—*To Lillian D. Clark, [8 June 1928]*

[Evanore Beebe's house in Wilbraham, Mass.] is full of odd rural lore, & ought to prove a mine of inspiration for any writer. I have already learned many things about old New England life previously known to me—such as the institution of *cat-ladders* inside the chimney of farmhouses, to enable the cats to climb from floor to floor when all the doors are shut. There is a fine system of cat ladders in this house—though only one ancient feline (Printer, aetat 17) knows how to use them. [. . .] Saturday better weather enabled me to take a walk through some of the picturesque country to the north, Mrs. Miniter serving as guide whilst both dogs *& one of the cats* acted as a quadrupedal retinue. I never before saw a cat which followed persons over hill & dale like a dog. [. . .] The *cats* all have different & highly individualised personalities—2 are grey (including a patriarch 17 years old) & five (including a very little kitten) are yellow.

—*To Lillian D. Clark, 1 July 1928*

I appreciate the feline quotation very much, & congratulate you upon so graceful a literary achievement. It amply fulfils the promise displayed in "We have toil'd among life's reapers." The sentiments are precisely suited to my tastes, & I recited it last night to my old black friend Calef-kittie as I paused to exchange greetings with him beside a colonial doorway in Thomas St. Calef-kittie grows younger as the years pass, & one beholds him higher & higher up the hill—& in greater & greater degrees of awakeness. I scarcely ever fail to see him now, & he knows the old gentleman very well; speaking to me in his own characteristic way as I pass toward down town & later pass back again. He & I are fellow-ancients—last reliques of 1848! I'd like to see one of those iron roof-cats you speak of. I vow, if I had one I'd entreat Miss Reynolds' permission to place him atop #10 Barnes!

—*To Annie E. P. Gamwell, 11 August [1928]*

If at this point my handwriting suddenly appears less legible, you may ascribe it to the self-invited presence of small tiger Hiram in his Grandpa's lap—for he has just jumped up there, & is trying to guide my pen with a velvet paw whilst he occasionally chews at the end of it between stentorian purrs. He is the friendliest little atom of fur & grace that I've ever seen in my life—indeed, he never enters the room without trotting straight to Grandpa & jumping up in the Old Gentleman's lap. When I am standing, he sometimes asks to be held, with a kind of amicable conversational mew. A great kitty—I certainly envy Orton the ability to harbour him. . . . Just now I heard the purring cease, & I find that the little rascal has fallen asleep. His head is on my right forearm, so I can move my wrist enough to write. Some tiger! [. . .] Hiram has just shifted in his sleep to a posture which makes writing more difficult, but I trust my epistle may still be read. [. . .] (Hiram has just changed his position & dropped off to sleep again. The new position makes writing somewhat easier.) [. . .] Hiram has waked up now & seems inclined to playfulness. The moving end of this pen arouses his interest most inordinately! No use talking—it takes a cat & an Old Farmer's Almanack to make a real home!

—To Lillian D. Clark, 20 April 1929

Having arriv'd [at W. Paul Cook's farm], I inspected the place in the charm of a golden twilight, & was duly transported. After a marvellous dinner I play'd with the new kitten, & later Munn came over in his dignified new car for a period of card-playing & congenial discussion. [. . .] The kitten spent much time in my lap—he is an exquisite atom only a few weeks old.

—To Lillian D. Clark, [17 May 1929]

But what interested me most of all at [W. Paul Cook's] farm were the *kitties*. The prettiest of them is a little tiger about ⅓ grown; but the most historically interesting is the full-grown cat which I saw as a tiny handful of fur last year when I visited Cook. You may recall my mentioning this specimen in my final bulletins from Athol on the former trip—Cook got it the very day I arrived, & it made its first trip to the old farm in my lap as I sat in Cook's old Whippet car. You may also recall how worried I was about its welfare when the Cooks accompanied me to Providence & left it locked in the house—& how relieved I was when Cook later wrote that he had called up Athol on the long distance telephone from Norwich to give instructions about its feeding. Well—little Togo (for so Mrs. Cook's 6-year-old grandson named him) is now a rather big Togo, but is still flourishing! He has had his accidents, though—including a 75-foot fall from a tree, which shook him up most painfully but did not injure him permanently. From his pleasant demeanour toward me I infer that he recognised the aged friend of his youth. Incidentally—my joy at finding Togo intact was somewhat offset by the news which Cook transmitted from the Beebe-Miniter farm in Wilbraham, where he visited last week. It seems that at least two of my seven furry friends there—the venerable Printer, born in 1911, & the scarcely less patriarchal Old Fats, who followed people about through the fields like a dog, having succumbed to the grim reaper's scythe at last. Eheu, fugaces! Old Printer was the last of an elder civilisation, & knew secret passages through the walls & up the chimney of the farmhouse (cf. my travel-letters, June 28–July 7, 1928) which none of the younger cats could ever discover! But speaking of cats—Munn has just obtained the most captivating little white kitten (with grey touches on head & tail) that I ever saw in my life! This exquisite little atom of purring & playfulness arrived on the very day that I did, (history thus repeating itself—since last year Cook got his kitten on the day that I arrived!) & has ever since formed the centre of interest in the Munn household. Kittie realises that Grandpa Theobald is very fond of his species, for he constantly makes for the Old Gentleman's lap & sleeps or kicks or chews there during long hours of reading, writing, & discussion. His adoptive family seem to appreciate him highly, & I trust he is destined for as long & honourable a life as Printer of Wilbraham, who rounded out 19 well-spent years.

—*To Lillian D. Clark, 12 June 1930*

I envy you the kitten—& in fact, all the cats. Cats are my favourite animals, my idolatry of them approaching that of the ancient Egyptians. Unfortunately I live in a single room & alcove, stacked with what is left of my family funiture & books, so that I cannot keep any pets. But if I had a regular house, the first accessory I would add to it would be a pert little black tom-kitten with large yellow eyes!

—*To R. H. Barlow, 13 October 1931*

Yes, indeed, I have often heard of the cat phobia—which is possessed to some extent by the wife of my friend Wilfred B. Talman. This type of phobia also exists in connexion with other animals—for example, the celebrated Renaissance astronomer Tycho Brahe was mortally afraid of a fox. Mrs. Talman isn't as bad a case as the one described in the cutting, but cats make her very nervous—so that Talman can't keep one despite his own fondness for them. I myself am an inveterate cat-lover—I'd have a dozen if there were any place to put them and any way to take convenient care of them.

—*To Robert E. Howard, 21 January 1933*

Yes—I shall have to write a Bubastian story some day—though I am always slow in getting around to any given plan. As a matter of fact I have fully half a dozen plots in mind that deal with the felidae.* One of the little kittens next door (which I think I mentioned to you) has been given away, & the other probably will be soon—but meanwhile the remaining one (which was the brighter one anyhow) is a marvellous little companion.

—*To Robert Bloch, [c. 22 August 1933]*

I was extremely fascinated by your description of your feline colleagues, & wish that I might see pictures of the nighted & saturnine Simaetha & the bluff & bellicose Genl. Tabasco. Simaetha would surely seem to be a true heir to the most sorcerous traditions of Hyperborea & Regio Averonum—not unlike those reputedly immortal felines who guarded the shrine of Sadoqua, & whose regular disappearances at New Moon figure so largely in the folklore of mediaeval Averoigne. One recalls the disquieting suggestions in Jehan d'Artois' Roman des Sorciers concerning the huge black cats captured at those very singular Sabbats on the rocky hill behind Vyones—the cats which could not be burned, but which escaped unhurt from the flames, uttering cries which, though not like any known human speech, were damnably close to the unknown syllables forming part of the Tsath-ritual in the Livre d'Eibon.

—*To Clark Ashton Smith, [c. 11 February 1934]*

There are four cats [in R. H. Barlow's household]—all delightful. A veteran white Tom named Doodle-Bug, & three little tigers named "High", "Low", & "Jack". My especial favourite is High—the darkest of the three—who trots like a little dog with

---

* HPL's commonplace book contains four such plots.

Barlow & me when we take our evening walks.
—*To Duane W. Rimel, 13 May 1934*

Incidentally—here are some snaps of the Barlovian scene which may interest you, & which you can add to your files if you like. They will shew up better if you magnify them as strongly as possible. In one of them you will see Grandpa (eyes closed inadvertently from sun-glare) holding a very nice distant cousin of Simaetha & Genl. Tabasco; & if you will study the background closely with a glass, you'll see good old Doodlebug gravely trotting into view. Another batch of views has gone forward to the Hyperborean High-Priestess E'ch-Vi-Es, with a request that they be brought before your eyes. Today the household is lamenting the vanishment of Jack, the largest of the younger Kappa Alpha Tau members, who has not been seen since yesterday morning, when he displayed signs of indisposition. I surely hope he'll turn up safely somehow! My particular friend, though, is the dark tiger "High"—who is on hand & in his customary lively health. [. . .] **Extra! Later!** Rejoicing in the Kappa Alpha Tau! *Jack has returned!* He shewed up at night, but with a curious weakness & lack of muscular coördination. He *staggers* oddly. It is possible that a snake bit him (damn Yig & all his spawn!), but I think the poison will work out & allow him to recover. He eats very sparingly & languidly, but purrs appealingly. If he doesn't recover, I'll have Two-Gun Bob come over here & eat all the local snakes alive!
—*To Clark Ashton Smith, [c. late May–early June 1934]*

In the view of "High" & myself I didn't notice that the former had also closed his eyes till you pointed it out. So old Doodle looks like your white cat? He is about three years old, but looks rather older & tougher than his age. He hunts a good deal, & goes off on long wilderness expeditions alone. I'll wager your cat is fascinating! The other day Jack (the larger tiger kitten) received a mysterious injury of some sort, & was lost for 36 hours. When he returned he shewed a tendency to stagger & lurch, & generally to lack muscular control. It is thought that a snake bit him. He is now growing stronger, & will probably pull through all right. [. . .] New anecdote of the returned Jack since I began this letter. He is stronger now, & upon being let out of the house made a bee line (despite his staggering) for a clump of palmettos near the lake. There he paused abruptly, raised his head, & began to purr loudly. Upon examining the clump we found a small dead snake with the head chewed up. This, without doubt, is the source of Jack's trouble. He must have caught & tried to eat the thing, & have been poisoned thereby. But what an ardent hunter to *remember* his prize & want to shew it off to the family! There's no question now but that he'll recover safely.

—*To Duane W. Rimel, 1 June 1934*

Glad the cat is coming along well—I'll be delighted to see a snap of him. By the way—my aunt tells me that there are more new kittens at the boarding-house across the back garden—which makes me rather anxious to get home. They'll probably be at a rather playful & interesting age when I arrive. Jack—down here—is almost well again, though he still has an odd tendency to carry his head on one side. He has taken to walking with us in the road like his brother High . . . . which Barlow discourages, for fear of accident from passing motors. [. . .] I agree about the intelligence, fine coördination, & independence of the cat—a great species! That tale of Blackwood's[*]

[*] "Ancient Sorceries," in *John Silence—Physician Extraordinary* (1908). It is a tale about the inhabitants of a small town in France, all of whom apparently turn into

was fascinating—& Carl Van Vechten reprinted it in his anthology of cat stories—"Lords of the Housetops." The apparent sensitiveness of your cat to intensive staring surely seems unusual, though I doubt if any messages can be transmitted save by the usual apparatus of the five senses. Coincidence is responsible for the average case of apparent telepathy.

—*To Duane W. Rimel, 17 June 1934*

The cats at De Land were all prospering when last I saw them; though one—Jack—has been through a trying experience. He was missing for a day, & when he turned up again he seemed curiously ill. All sense of balance was gone, & he lurched & staggered like a feline toper! As he grew stronger, he seemed anxious to visit a neighbouring clump of palmettoes near the lake—where, it was discovered, lay a small snake . . . dead, & with a somewhat tooth-mangled cranium. Undoubtedly Jack had chosen this reptile for his prey, & had become poisoned by his ophidian feast. He's coming out all right, though. Of the little 'possums, only one managed to survive for any length of time, & even he succumbed in the end. He received the name of Henry, & graduated long before his demise from medicine-dropper nutritive methods. At another place in De Land I saw the most exquisite black kitten—a tiny atom, but wildly playful—that can be imagined.

—*To Elizabeth Toldridge, 21 June 1934*

Thanks tremendously for the feline cuttings! I can see that the Atlantic coast has no monopoly on notable kinsfolk of the jungle's lords . . . . as indeed was made apparent before through descriptions of the felidae of Woods' Dry Diggings.* Lord Cats-

cats at night.

* The original name of Auburn, Cal., before the town was renamed in the 1849 gold rush.

paw & the Messrs Johnson are all obviously gentlemen of quality, & I trust the matter of social procedure amongst them may soon be settled with honour & satisfaction to all. Slushfoot's snow-white progeny are certainly remarkable indeed—& would appear to have a link of common ancestry with Doodlebug. By the way—Barlow manor expects an increase in its furry population through the agency of the little tigress "Low", & the probabilities are that at least one or two of the newcomers will possess something of old Doodlebug's snowiness. Jack, I am pleased to say (he will be "Uncle Jack" when the new generation arrives!), is now as well as ever, though he still carries his head slightly on one side as a reminder of his painful experience. I guess I told you how he mewingly led the family down to a clump of palmettoes near the lake, where reposed a dead snake with chewed-up head. Undoubtedly he tried to eat something that wasn't good for him! ¶ Those infant bobcats are fascinating, & I'll wager their owner will hate to turn them over to the zoo. I'd try to keep them—didn't the Romans have pet leopards?

—To Clark Ashton Smith, [25 June 1934]

Incidentally, I hope Jack & everybody are flourishing. Any kittens yet? I saw the most fascinating imaginable single handful of black & white purring fur at the local bus station this morning. Had to stop a quarter-hour & play with it. Reminded me of the lamented Nicolo at the Shell Mound!

—To R. H. Barlow, 29 June 1934

And so the kittens are yellow & brindle! Poor Doodle must feel quite disconcerted! Sorry they didn't arrive in time for me to see them. Will all be retained? If not, I hope they'll find good homes. [. . .] How is Jack's neck these days?

—To R. H. Barlow, 12 July 1934

Regarding a name for your splendid snow-white beast, I fancy the Arctic suggestions of his colour might serve as a guide. He could be one of the frosty gods of our old Northern ancestors—Odin, Thor, Freyr, Ymir, Loki, & so on . . . . or you could name him *Crom,* after the icy deity of Bob Howard's mythical "Cimmeria". "Polaris" wouldn't be a bad monicker—& if you wanted to go to the *antarctic* for your snowy whiteness, you could call him "Tekeli-li" after the cry of the bird in the white polar world of Poe's "Arthur Gordon Pym".

—*To Duane W. Rimel, 10 August 1934*

I learn with pleasure of [Crom's] growth & prosperity, & am interested in your account of his diet & habits. A fine boy, & with a distinct individuality of his own! I shall indeed be glad to see a more recent picture of him—& will shew it to President Randall (black & white) & Vice-President Osterberg (tiger) of the K.A.T. I feel confident that they will ensure his election as an honorary member!

—*To Duane W. Rimel, 8 October 1934*

Coincidence regarding feline disasters has surely reached a malign maximum—for lo! Sad advices from Charles Johnston in De Land* tell of the vanishment of the venerable white Doodlebug whose photographic likeness you have beheld! He disappeared three weeks ago; & in view of the ophidian population of the district, very little hope is now entertained. This will be a bad blow for little Ar-E'ch-Bei when the news reaches him in Washington! Now I suppose High & Jack will be candidates for the presidency of the De Land chapter of the Kappa Alpha Tau! But the existence of others' woes does not lighten one's own—hence I extend the fullest measure of sympathy regard-

---

* The Barlows' hired hand. A few postcards from HPL to him survive.

ing the swallowing up of General Tabasco by the vast void! Good old warrior! And just as I was hoping to see a likeness of him! One is still tempted to hope that some miracle may bring him back. If not, may he have met his end as a true fighter should, with a high ring of the slain around his dying form. What Entities he may have faced on his last field of action, none may tell—but I feel sure they must have been far more formidable than any mere spawn of earth. Perhaps the Nameless Eikon hints a clue—now that I turn to view it, it seems to harbour an unwonted leer. I marvel not that Mother Simaetha mourns in desolation. Tell her to use her darkest arts in divining & withering the curst hidden power whereby the hero fell. Outside my window the elders of the K.A.T. shake their heads in sympathy. I shall consult with them—especially with the valiant Count Magnus—on possible measures of divination & reprisal!

—To Clark Ashton Smith, [28 October 1934]

Well—though Doodlebug has not returned to the Villa Barlovia, something very like him has marched into Price's new home on a Redwood City hilltop. Crom has a rival for the pure white championship of the Pacific Coast, for this newcomer . . . an utterly strange, gigantic tom who appeared from nowhere . . . . is a mighty hunter & warrior indeed! His capacity for food exceeds all previously known bounds, while his belligerency is worthy of Conan the Reaver. The other day he clawed a gopher out of its hole & brought it for his master to see before devouring it . . . . . & more recently he attacked & routed a huge strange dog who had eyed his bowl of beans too calculatively. In view of his prowess in the chase, Sultan Malik has named him Nimrod, & he has been duly recognised as overlord of all the California chapters of the Kappa Alpha

Tau . . . though of course General Tabasco might challenge his supremacy if he saw fit to return to the Temple of Tsathogua in Averoigne. So Crom is settling down in size! Glad he has such a fine, heavy coat—& hope he will soon recover his former industriousness in the matter of keeping it snowy. Turning to the other end of the chromatic scheme—there are 4 little niggers at the boarding-house across the garden from old 66—brothers or half-brothers of the late & unforgottable Sam Perkins. Frantic telephonic attempts are being made to find good homes for them, though I fervently hope at least one will be kept as a successor to little Sam.

—*To Duane W. Rimel, 10 March 1935*

I guess I told you of Sultan Malik's new home & white hunting-leopard . . . . the latter a veritable Doodlebug plus ferocity & appetite. Nimrod lately attacked a huge dog who was gazing too speculatively at his bowl of beans, & has developed a penchant for riding with his master in Juggernaut. If the Peacock Sultan takes him along on his visit to Klarkash-Ton, old Mother Simaetha will need all the protective sorceries inherited from a long line of ancestors in Bubastis & Meroë.

—*To H. R. Barlow, [16 March 1935]*

Nimrod valiantly fights the gophers that nibble at their roots—& to aid in the battle the Sultan is going to get the dauntless warrior a harem of 3 or 4 furry ladies—who, together with the future Nimrodic heirs, will probably be able to exterminate the whole colony of burrowers. Nimrod's prowess—& appetite—continue unabated . . . & no rival is likely to stand much chance in the annual election of the California chapter of the K.A.T.! No word, alas, from Genl. Tabasco . . . . or from Doodlebug! [. . .] Congratulations to Crom upon his children! Hope they'll all prosper & do their noble sire proper credit! Glad the snowy paterfamilias is prospering, & hope he'll continue to dominate the Washington chapter of the K.A.T. White seems to be a favourite colour with K.A.T. leaders—what with Crom, Nimrod, & the vanished Doodlebug! The Providence chapter is duly responding to the call of spring—& I had an excellent talk with Pres. Randall yesterday afternoon. Of the little niggers across the garden *one* remains—& oh, boy, what an one! Meet Mr. John Perkins, successor to & near-double of the late lamented Sam! Is he a little streak of playful black lightning? Just like little Sam—except that he has a tiny white shirt-stud visible on close inspection. His eyes still have the violet wideness of infancy, but he is strong & active—& has just begun to *purr.* I think he is larger & stronger than Sam at the same age—& I certainly hope he'll survive & flourish! He has visited me several times—& I play with him with a stick of which his late brother was especially fond. He is just beginning to assimilate other than maternal nourishment.

—To Duane W. Rimel, 16 April 1935

More bad news for K.A.T. Rimel's snow-white Crom—after being exiled across the river because of alleged poultry depredations—has joined that mysterious company of the vanish'd to which Gen. Tabasco & Doodlebug already belong. Possibly the Peacock Sultan has told you of valiant Nimrod's 6-day disappearance. Down here in the jungle there are rumours that old Dood is still alive—gone native & roaming the steaming swamps in savage & uninhibited splendour. In Providence Mr. John Perkins is getting to be a peppy black devil—so martial in habits as to form a problem among the local felidae. He was a visitor of mine most days until my departure on the present visit.

—To Clark Ashton Smith, [16 June 1935]

I mourn for the lost Crom! The Kappa Alpha Tau, en masse, mourns with me! And Mr. John Perkins, whose rather unfavourably snapped likeness you'll find amidst the enclosed photographs, adds his plaintive & still juvenile "eeew" to the melancholy chorus. What evil is this which stalks the leaders of the K.A.T., & spans an entire continent with its cryptic malevolence? I have referred the matter to Nimrod, valiant snow-white warrior-chieftain of Many-Pillared Irem, & hope that he will bend all his savage energies toward the extermination of the Unknown Adversary. Enclosed, by the way, is a recent photograph of that Conan among Quadrupeds—in the arms of the invincible Peacock Sultan. Well—you certainly have my unalloyed sympathy! Damn & double-damn the meddlesome idiots whose complaints caused his banishment to uncongenial soil! Iä! Shub-Niggurath! May his alabaster-white sons wax great & vengeful, & sally forth to exterminate all the poultry of the mendacious dastards! Anyhow, I hope you'll acquire one of these sturdy heirs. In the interim, pray extend my greetings to the little grey fellow—who may be regarded as the Regent of the Northwestern Kappa Alpha Tau until the heir of Crom comes to reigning age. Yea—there is surely a new monarch in Ablakar . . . to whom is given the Lordship of the Middle Kingdom, betwixt the lands of his snowy cousin Doodlebug & his duskier fellow-Westerner General Tabasco. To his court shall ofttimes stray Little Sam Perkins, ever young & playful, & legions of other furry companions lost to earth. Hail & farewell, O Crom . . . . . mighty shall be thy memory in Cimmeria! [. . .] There is a pleasing report that old white Doodlebug is *not dead*—but that he has 'gone native' & is joyously roaming the subtropical jungle. Many rumours of a strange white cat—glimpsed fleetingly by the roadside— have become current along the countryside.

—*To Duane W. Rimel, 30 June 1935*

I'm interested by the news of the feline population, and wish I could see some of the furry specimens enumerated. Too bad Mubsy is so self-sacrificing on the food question! In its present well-fed shape, the family must be a delight to see—and I hope the kittens' eyes will soon respond to the botic acid treatment. The way the various mothers pool their kittens is surely picturesque. The stray kitten must be quite a fellow if he can catch milk squirted directly from the cow! Greedy is surely an active young Casanova! [. . .] As for the felidae [at R. H. Barlow's house]—Doodlebug (the snow-white patriarch) vanished last autumn, but there are rumours of his being alive and roaming the neighbourhood jungle in a wild state. High has seceded from the Barlow fold and joined the Johnstons at Dunover, but is still as friendly as ever. Low has been given away—while Jack, his neck still a trifle stiff from his snake-bite experience of last year, is the dean of the outdoors cats. Henry Clay and Alfred A. Knopf (yellow and grey spotted, respectively) are kittens of Low's, and permanent additions to the extra-mural menage. Within the house are two lordly and pedigreed Persians brought down from Washington by Bob. Of these one—Cyrus—is extremely playful and affectionate, while the other—Darius—is as yet haughty and aloof, though he exhibits subtle signs of mellowing. Cyrus and Darius are yellow in hue, and look precisely alike. They are full brothers.
—*To Robert E. Howard, 11 July 1935*

The visit [to R. H. Barlow's house in De Land, Florida] somewhat parallels last year's, except that Little Bobby's papa is now at home. [. . .] Of the felidae, old Doodlebug & High have vanish'd, whilst Jack flourishes with a neck only slightly awry from last year's snake bite. Low has been given to a grocery store in Eustis, but her two kittens Henry Clay (yellow) & Alfred A. Knopf (tiger) remain as permanent additions to the flock. And besides all these there are two lordly & pamper'd Persians—Cyrus & Darius—whom Bobby brought down from Washington.

—*To James F. Morton, 21 July 1935*

I mourn afresh at Crom's continued absence—& to think his sons & his grey successor have likewise vanished into the mists of Aklakar! Here's hoping you have better luck with the little black boy—perhaps your change of residence will help to break the evil spell. If misery loves company, here's some bad news to cheer you up—*High & Jack have both disappeared within the last fortnight.* It is pretty well agreed, however, that they are not dead. Cats have a tendency to revert to wild nature in this region—inhabitants of backwoods cottages reporting whole troops of them in the jungle. Probably High, Jack, & old white Doodlebug are all alive & enjoying themselves as free men—emancipated for ever from servitude to the whims of the irrational biped *homo sapiens.* Back at #66 little Johnny Perkins is growing up to be a formidable fighting man—even attempting at times to intimidate the august elders of the Kappa Alpha Tau. He has a little black & white sister or half-sister now—who looks just like their mother, & who will be given away as soon as she is able to leave the maternal bosom. She may be gone before my return—but I trust Johnny will be on hand to give the old gentleman a cordial & purring welcome. Well—let us hope that the little black boy at Asotin will grow up plump, valiant, & wise, & in time be ready to take his place as Supreme Regent of the Kappa Alpha Tau's Northwestern Chapter. Just south of you, Nimrod is prospering in accustomed fashion—despite various mysterious absences as long as 5 & 6 days each. He goes on dark & cryptic quests—but always comes back. Sultan Malik now has a second feline at the many-pillar'd palace of Irem—a tiny yellow kitten, tiger-striped, with whom old Nim is reluctantly making friends. May they all live long & flourish!

—To Duane W. Rimel, 4 August 1935

By the way—I'm obliged to record two more local feline disappearances . . . I told you that old Doodlebug vanished last winter. Within the past month both High and Jack (the latter the hero of last year's snake encounter) have followed the snowy patriarch into the realm of obscurity—though natives assure us that all three are probably still alive and flourishing. Reversions of cats to a wild state are common in Florida—dwellers in remote places telling of legions of them seen and heard in the woods at night. The Barlovian felidae are now reduced to four—Henry Clay (yellow) and Alfred A. Knopf (tiger) outdoors, and Cyrus and Darius (yellow Persians) indoors. Up at the Johnston cottage are two more—San Marcos (tiger) and San Sebastian (yellow). Henry, Alfred, Marcos, and Sebastian are all kittens of Low—who has been given to a grocery store in Eustis. The two saints are of the summer '34 crop, whilst Henry and Alfred were born last winter. It is curious that both of Low's litters consisted of 2 male kittens—one yellow and one tiger. She herself is tiger. Back in Providence my little black friend Johnny Perkins is getting to be a formidable fighting man—menacing the peace of the quiet Elders of the Kappa Alpha Tau. He can put old Pres. Randall to flight just by arching his back and hissing—but valiant Mr. Osterberg is less easily daunted. Johnny has a little white-and-black sister now—but she will probably be given away as soon as she is able to leave the maternal bosom. I'll certainly be glad to see Mr. Perkins in my return. My aunt says he comes to call quite frequently—curling up and purring in his favourite chair.

—To Robert E. Howard, 7 August 1935

Glad to hear of the fast-growing little nigger at Box 100! I think *Sotho* would be a most appropriate name for him . . . as a cryptic daemon allied to the vast, engulfing, & immemorial night. [. . .] Glad Sotho likes his new home. I still mourn the vanished Crom, & hope he may be roaming jungles of wonder & beauty with all his accustomed grace. The whereabouts of Doodlebug, Gen. Tabasco, High, & Jack remain equally shrouded in mystery.

— *To Duane W. Rimel, 28 September 1935*

Regards to Sotho—both from me & from the drowsy mountain of black fur which purrs intermittently in the semicircular chair on my left! I'd surely like to see a picture of the little imp of darkness when you get a good one. I can imagine the texture of his coat. Johnny Perkins's is also of that intense, glistening, unvaried, & almost bluish lustre—in contrast to his later brother Sam's, which revealed faint traces of a latent tiger heredity. Glad Sotho & his pa get on well together—I'll bet the old gentleman is proud of his boy! Johnny's (& I think Sam's) father is a lean, restless gentleman of the neighbourhood; coal-black, & rather reluctant to make friends with the human species. Johnny has certain characteristic postures which precisely duplicate those of his 1934 brother. Well—to make up for bereavements, Johnny now has 3 new little brothers (or sisters, or both—I don't know), for all of whom good homes have been found. One coal-black, two black & white. They will be delightful companions until the time comes to deliver them to their respective new abodes. Johnny spends a good deal of his time over here, & seems to appreciate the catnip he gets. (Catnip also grows wild in New England, but I don't know of any place to find it.) No further Kappa Alpha Tau disasters in Providence—or in De Land at last reports. Here's hoping that both Sotho & Mr. Perkins may grow into patriarchs as venerable as Old Man & Pres. Peter Randall!

—To Duane W. Rimel, 12 November 1935

The Providence chapter of the K.A.T. extends its most cordial regards to Sotho & his sire. Johnny Perkins's little brothers are now divided—two given away, & one (a fascinating black-&-white devil who doesn't seem to mind Johnny's cuffing him around) still here. I shall hate to see the dispersal completed. The old patriarchs of the shed roof aren't seen much now that the weather is colder, though the tiger vice-president shews himself briefly now & then.

—To Duane W. Rimel, 15 December 1935

Thanks for the feline-canine article—which I heartily endorse, & to which my black friend Mr. John Perkins (b. Feby. 14, 1935, now a huge & mighty hunter) purrs his most enthusiastic approval. Here is that article I spoke about—which you might return eventually. It looks pretty flamboyant & immature today, & I feel abashed to reflect that I was writing such tripe only a decade ago. However, you must remember that it was largely a personal matter—meant for the perusal of a club from which I had but lately withdrawn because of my return to Providence from Brooklyn. Morton told me about the cat-&-dog programme, & asked me to send him something to read at the meeting. This was the result—though the personal Mortonian & Blue Pencil slant sounds odd to one not in close touch with the group. Yuggoth, what reams of utterly pointless & futile tripe I have ground out in the course of a long lifetime!

—To R. H. Barlow, 11 March 1936

Glad, too, that Sotho takes kindly to the change. Your tailless neighbour ought to make a good friend for Sotho. Are you sure his caudal deficiency is *artificial?* As you know, the Manx cat is naturally tailless—& many cats in America have Manx strains. When I visited my ancestral region in western Rhode Island in 1926 & 1929 I was impressed by the prevalence of tailless cats there. Evidently a Manx litter were imported there some time in the last 60 years, so that the local feline population is thickly permeated with the strain.

—To Duane W. Rimel, 20 June 1936

Sorry to hear of the death of Sotho's new companion. Some hellish cosmic force seems to be an enemy of the Kappa Alpha Tau! By the way—it is *not* in *Providence* cats that a tailless Manx strain exists, but in the cats of the western Rhode Island countryside where my maternal ancestors came from. The times I particularly noticed this peculiarity were in 1926 & 1929, when I visited the region in question.

—To Duane W. Rimel, 27 August 1936

I learn with genuine sorry [*sic*] & dismay of Sotho's vanishment. If he does not turn up eventually, I shall suspect some especially potent league of malign powers against the Kappa Alpha Tau! Crom . . . Nimrod . . . Doodlebug . . . . Sam & Johnny Perkins . . . Lord Minto . . . General Tabasco . . . . I shall ask Klarkash-Ton to have the venerable Mother Simaetha invoke a particularly potent counter-curse at the coming Hallowmass Sabbat! Incidentally—Sultan Malik has a fine new member for the Redwood City Chapter of the K.A.T. . . . . a coal-black young gentleman 4 months of age, known as "Pot-Likker", & a half-brother to the already-installed tiger member known variously as Ki-Ki, Battle-Axe, & the Conquering Lion of Judah. With the intermediation of Battle-Axe, I fancy the new-comer will be taught to carry on the noble martial traditions of the lost Nimrod.

—*To Duane W. Rimel, 24 October 1936*

Commiserations on Sotho's continued absence—the remnants of the K.A.T.'s Providence Chapter transmit their sincere & mournful miaows! My previous bulletin has told you of the similar blow sustained by the Redwood City chapter—indeed, the past few years have dealt the mighty fraternity some lethal strokes all over the country! We must call some sort of convention of witches & sorcerers like Mother Simaetha to invoke fresh & additionally potent forms of retributive magic against the Outer Things whose ravages have been so cruel!

—*To Duane W. Rimel, 20 December 1936*

October 20 & 21 were phenomenally warm, & I utilised them in exploring a hitherto untapped region down the east shore of Narragansett Bay where the Barrington Parkway winds along the lofty bluff above the water. It is, in general, the area to the right of our usual route to Aunt Julia's. I found a highly fascinating forest called the Squantum Woods—where there are great oaks & birches, steep slopes & rock ledges, & breath-taking westward vistas beyond the trees. On both occasions there was a fine sunset—then glimpses of the crescent moon, Venus, & Jupiter . . . & the lights of far-off Providence from high places along the parkway. On my expedition of the 20th a particularly congenial bodyguard or retinue attended me through the sunlit arcades of the grove—in the persons of *two tiny kittens*, one gray & one tortoise-shell, who appeared out of nowhere in the midst of the sylvan solitudes. Blithe spirits of the ancient wood—furry faunlets of the shadowy vale! I wonder where their mother was? Judging by their diminutiveness, they could scarce have been fully graduated from her as a source of nourishment. Probably they appertained to an hospital whose grounds are contiguous with the mystical forest. Both were at first very timid, & reluctant to let Grandpa catch them; but eventually the little grey fellow became very purr-ful & amicable—climbing over the old gentleman, playing with twigs & with Grandpa's watch-charm, & eventually curling up & going to sleep in the grandpaternal lap. But Little Brother remained suspicious & aloof—clawing & spitting with surprising vehemence on the one occasion when Grandpa caught him. He hung around, however, because he didn't want to lose his brother! Not wishing to wake my new friend, I carried him about when I continued my ramble—Little Tortoise-Shell Brother tagging along reluctantly & dubiously at a discreet distance in the rear. When the grey faunlet awaked, he requested to be set down; but proceeded to trot companionably after Grandpa—sometimes getting under the old gentleman's feet & considerably retarding progress. Thus I roamed the venerable forest aisles for an hour & a half—till the ruddy disc of the sun vanished behind the farther hills. As I emerged from the wood, I feared that my faithful retinue might follow me on to the broad parkway & incur the perils of motor traffic—and was considering expedients (such as putting Little Grey Boy a short distance up a tree) for discouraging their further attendance—but discovered that they were not without native caution. Or perhaps they were wholly genii loci, without real existence apart from their dim nemorense habitat. At any rate, Little Grey Boy paused at the edge of the grove with a mewed farewell—& naturally Little Tortoise-Shell had no great eagerness to follow. I bade them a regretful & ceremonious adieu—& on the next day looked for them in vain.

—To James F. Morton, [December 1936–January 1937]

By this time you have my Yuletide epistle telling of salient holiday events & gifts hereabouts, & thanking you most sincerely for the sleeping figurine of my late friend & neighbour John Perkins. The more I look at that statuette, the more its grace & naturalness appeals to me. You have certainly caught the exquisitely distinctive lines of feline relaxation—not for nothing have you been the friend & associate of noble beasts like Doodle Bug, High, Low, Jack, Henry Clay, Cyrus, Darius, & Little Mr. Knopf! It is interesting to know that this is your first effort in the given medium—a decided success, if you ask me! Sleeping Johnny Perkins certainly makes a fine showing among the other gifts—which include a group of two very diminutive cat figures, a card with a whole Kappa Alpha Tau personnel peering over a fence, & a daily calendar with three delightful black kittens on it. Santa obviously knew the Old Gent's tastes!

—To R. H. Barlow, 3 January [1937]

What a boy he [Nigger-Man] was! I watched him grow from a tiny black handful to one of the most fascinating & understanding creatures I've ever seen. He used to talk in a genuine language of varied intonation—a special tone for every different meaning. There was even a special "prrr'p" for the smell of roast chestnuts, on which he doted. He used to play ball with me—kicking a large rubber sphere back at me from half across the room with all four feet as he lay on the floor. And on summer evenings in the twilight he would prove his kinship to the elfin things of shadow by racing across the lawn on nameless errands, darting into the blackness of the shrubbery now & then, & occasionally leaping at me from ambush & then bounding away again into invisibility before I could catch him.

—To Harry O. Fischer, 10 January 1937

Felis: A Prose Poem

by Frank Belknap Long

Oh, how delightful it is to stroke the sinuous hair of felicitous cats. Long, long ago I discovered that these happy creatures know more than Adam our father because they have never been tempted by the evil one, have never eaten of the forbidden fruit and have never fallen. I know that in their great, fearless, seductive eyes there lurk sinister secrets, preincarnate hieroglyphics which only the gods can fathom, secrets and signs which portend nothing but evil for man. And they are immortal; you cannot kill them. When the tiny sphere which certain weary seers have agreed to call the earth, for lack of a better name, shall have permitted itself to become cold through sheer ennui there shall yet remain the cats. They are immortal and shall live always, even as the old stone gods, even as the voluptuous Venus, even as the albino and implacable Delphic Apollo. Long have I studied them, and I have become, in a degree, their slave. They have begun to exercise an unholy fascination over me and have even stolen into my dreams, into the secret chambers of my fancy. I shall always see them now, whenever I dream, large and sinewy and soft with prismatic eyes, scintillating eyes, vacillating eyes, eyes green and blue, and pale, washed-out yellow, like the mournful orbs of the melancholy Kakue bird of Paraguay who possesses the immortal soul of a negress. And in my dreams they climb over my arms and legs and purr and whine disconsolately. And when I reach out, fascinated, and smooth their long fur I experience a joy at once profound and awful—*because their fur is soft and burns my fingers.* There is something *outré* about their fur. I have seen great waste places entirely inhabited by cats. I have seen cats of all colors, of all shades, of all hues, and of every shape and size. I have seen shrunken cats and cats with elephantiasis and deformed and misshapen and dwarfed cats. I have seen cats that could talk and cats that could laugh and, yes, I have actually seen a cat who could dance. But whenever I dream of cats I see the spiced mummy of some august Pharaoh, or a skeleton rider carrying a scythe riding furiously around an ever widening circle or a radiant corpse swinging gracefully under a cloudless blue sky. When I walk the streets of our great cities I am haunted by cats. I see them everywhere, behind the smooth glass of costly limousines, on street corners, in the languid eyes of women, by deserted waterfronts, in the smoke of a man's pipe, on top of tall buildings, down dark and unfrequented alleys, and in the pale yellow light of the city's gas lamps. Some day I shall drown in a sea of cats. I shall go down, smothered by their embraces, feeling their warm breath upon my face, gazing into their large eyes, hearing in my ears their soft purring. I shall sink lazily down through oceans of fur, between myriads of claws, clutching innumerable tails, and I shall surrender my wretched soul to the selfish and insatiable god of felines.